"With a myriad of books on leadership add[...] the book for which I have been waiting [...] not only reinforces the essential calling of followership but rightly makes a persuasive and compelling biblical case that leadership's most intimate companion is followership. A paradox of effective leadership is that to lead well we must follow well. I could not recommend this book more highly for all apprentices of Jesus who long to live a faithful and fruitful life."

**Tom Nelson,** Senior Pastor, Christ Community Church, Kansas City; President, Made to Flourish; author, *Work Matters* and *The Economics of Neighborly Love*

"Everyone wants to lead; few want to follow. Turns out that Jesus was a follower. He did the work his heavenly Father gave him to do. It's time to follow his lead in relationships, in marriages, and in our work worlds. Joanne Jung and Richard Langer address a topic no one wants to tackle in our leader-crazed culture. Don't worry, this is not a pedantic primer on followership. It includes a practical section, 'Soul Rhythms for Faithful Following', that will jump-start your followership skills. If you love leading and bristle at following, follow my lead and put this book on your list."

**Greg Leith,** CEO, Convene

"It turns out that great leaders have great lieutenants. Jesus himself is a consummate follower—of the Father. Langer and Jung wisely point out that following can be dangerous, even deadly; lemmings and cliffs come to mind. So they don't advocate *blind* following—the blind *following* the blind—but offer strong exhortations to wise and courageous following, which comes down to a matter of heart and pays lasting fruit. Their chart contrasting followership stereotypes with biblical followership is worth the price of the book."

**Sam Crabtree,** Pastor for Small Groups, Bethlehem Baptist Church; author, *Practicing Thankfulness*

"Langer and Jung provide a clarion call for the church to take followership seriously. They present a refreshing vision of biblical followership and remind readers that mission-centric and faithful obedience is what sets people apart whether they are leaders or followers. The book puts followership and leadership in proper perspective and offers timeless principles and examples for believers to be faithful Christ followers."

**John Shoup,** Executive Director, Dr. Paul & Annie Kienel Leadership Institute; Professor of Leadership Studies, California Baptist University

"*The Call to Follow* is such a refreshing read that relieves leaders of the pressure of working harder to lead better. I've been waiting for a book like this! What if we just spent time thinking about following Jesus, pure and simple? Joanne Jung and Richard Langer, my dear Biola University colleagues, remind us all in these pages that we are best when following, not to be more effective leaders but to be more faithful disciples. This book is a true gift to Jesus followers, which is all we need to be. We may move in and out of leadership, but there is never a day when we will not be followers. We are 'disciples' of Christ, a term that means followers. We have no higher aspiration than to follow the author and perfecter of our faith."

**Barry H. Corey,** President of Biola University; author, *Love Kindness: Discover the Power of a Forgotten Christian Virtue*

"I am grateful to have a work in hand that focuses on following for the sake of serving rather than seeking to eventually lead. Langer and Jung reveal the repeated theological, cruciform importance of God-fearing followership to the mission of Christ and his kingdom. Local congregations and Christian ministries will be dramatically influenced and empowered for congregational-maturing and neighborhood-transforming good works if they recover this vision for biblical followership. May we accept this invitation to embrace the soul rhythms that beautify our callings to be followers."

**Eric C. Redmond,** Professor of Bible, Moody Bible Institute

*The Call to Follow*

# The Call to Follow

*Hearing Jesus in a Culture Obsessed with Leadership*

Richard Langer and Joanne J. Jung

Foreword by Gavin Ortlund

**:: CROSSWAY®**

WHEATON, ILLINOIS

---

**Library of Congress Cataloging-in-Publication Data**

Names: Jung, Joanne J., author. | Langer, Richard, author.
Title: The call to follow : hearing Jesus in a culture obsessed with leadership / Joanne J Jung and Richard Langer.
Description: Wheaton, Illinois : Crossway, 2022. | Includes bibliographical references and index.
Identifiers: LCCN 2021048713 (print) | LCCN 2021048714 (ebook) | ISBN 9781433578038 (trade paperback) | ISBN 9781433578045 (pdf) | ISBN 9781433578052 (mobipocket) | ISBN 9781433578069 (epub)
Subjects: LCSH: Christian life. | Followership. | Leadership.
Classification: LCC BV4509.5 .J85 2022 (print) | LCC BV4509.5 (ebook) | DDC 248.4–dc23/eng/20211118
LC record available at https://lccn.loc.gov/2021048713
LC ebook record available at https://lccn.loc.gov/2021048714

---

Crossway is a publishing ministry of Good News Publishers.

| VP | | 30 | 29 | 28 | 27 | 26 | 25 | 24 | 23 | 22 |
|----|----|----|----|----|----|----|----|----|----|----|
| 14 | 13 | 12 | 11 | 10 | 9 | 8 | 7 | 6 | 5 | 4 | 3 | 2 | 1 |

# Contents

Foreword    *9*

Acknowledgments    *13*

Introduction    *15*

1   Of Leading and Following    *23*

2   Mistaken Beliefs about Followership    *37*

3   A Kingdom of Followers    *59*

4   A Crisis of Followership    *77*

5   Glimpses of Faithful Following    *109*

6   Still I Will Follow    *129*

7   Soul Rhythms for Faithful Following    *149*

8   The Rewards of Following    *175*

Conclusion    *191*

Study Guide    *195*

General Index    *215*

Scripture Index    *219*

# Foreword

I READ A STATISTIC recently about how many pastors would leave the ministry if they could. I won't tell you what it was. It would probably be a bit of a downer to start a book like that! But the figure was high. The sad reality is that right now many pastors are discouraged and many churches are in decline or crisis.

While there are obviously many factors contributing to this situation, an important one may be an overemphasis on leadership.

Overemphasis on leadership? Did you read that right? Yes, you did. It may sound strange, but the fact is that leadership is often misunderstood, idolized, overvalued, or uncritically pursued. This problem pervades our culture and, unfortunately, affects the church as well.

Rick Langer and Joanne Jung have written an enormously helpful, wise, and important book to help us address this problem. Langer and Jung do not deny the goodness or importance of leadership—far from it! But they show how certain ways of thinking about leadership can be from the flesh, not the Spirit. It is so easy for worldliness to creep in right in the midst of our efforts to advance the kingdom of heaven. Yet, our methods as well as our message must *follow* the way of Christ—and that includes how we think about leadership.

Langer and Jung show that in order to understand leadership, we must understand *followership*. Followership is often misunderstood and undervalued. (Just think of how rarely the word "followership" is used!) Followership does not mean uncritical passivity or weakness. It is not less noble than leadership. It is not less valuable. It is not even less difficult. On the contrary, followership is a rewarding, honorable, and fulfilling aspect of both our humanity and our spirituality.

When you think about it, the importance of followership is a matter of common sense. If there are no followers, then by definition no one can be a leader. That means that if everyone is striving for leadership, everyone will be frustrated *in* that leadership. Thus, when we teach our people that "everyone is a leader," we are setting ourselves up for problems. All institutional health depends on give-and-take, complementary roles of leadership and responsiveness.

As Langer and Jung demonstrate, followership is essential to the flourishing of all human institutions, but it is especially imperative in the church. After all, we worship a man who said, "If anyone would come after me, let him deny himself and take up his cross and *follow* me" (Mark 8:34). Followership is at the heart of being a Christian. We are the sheep; he is the shepherd. Thus, for Christians, followership is primary and essential, while leadership is derivative. We are *all* called to cultivate the skills and virtues associated with following. Some of us will also be called into roles of leadership; but when we are, our leadership will only be effective to the extent we are *following* Christ.

True leadership is not superior to followership; it flows out of followership.

Just consider what a huge factor this is for the flourishing of our churches! How might our churches be healthier and more cohesive if they were filled with people who intentionally valued following? How many difficult membership meetings would go more smoothly? How many ministries would function more fruitfully? How many pastors and elders would find sudden wind in their sails? How many more people would hear about Jesus in our communities?

*The Call to Follow: Hearing Jesus in a Culture Obsessed with Leadership* is a word in season. Langer and Jung point to helpful models of leadership and followership, such as Abraham Kuyper's relationship with his local church members (see chap. 5). They give practical advice on how to cultivate healthy habits of followership. And they show how cultivating the virtues necessary to be a follower of Christ is not a burden but actually the key to finding rest for our souls. If Christians take to heart this counsel, our churches will be both healthier and happier—to the glory of God.

*Gavin Ortlund*
SENIOR PASTOR, FIRST BAPTIST CHURCH OF OJAI
OJAI, CALIFORNIA

# Acknowledgments

THIS BOOK WAS BORN in a hallway. It sounds strange but it is true. Without a whole series of tiny conversations that took place in the hallway that connects our offices, Joanne and I would never have had a few big conversations; without a few big conversations, we would never have realized that we had a whole book's worth of things we wanted to say about leading and following. We are keenly aware of the blessing of hallways because we were both at Biola University during many years when the Bible department was scattered between seven different buildings. It was a time before hallways—a time with far fewer of the tiny conversations that are the seeds of the bigger ones.

So we offer a heartfelt acknowledgment to many donors who made the Talbot East Building at Biola University possible. Without those donors, there would have been no building, no hallway, and no book. Your generosity has truly been a blessing to us and, we hope, a blessing to the many people who will read this book.

# Introduction

OUR CULTURE PROMOTES LEADERSHIP in myriad contexts—
sports teams and clubs for elementary-aged children, campus clubs
for junior high students and high schoolers, degree programs for
college students, and more. Professional schools, whether in business, law, medicine, or theology, all offer extensive training in leadership. Once our prospective leaders have graduated, they continue
their leadership pursuits in the marketplace with countless programs for identifying potential leaders and developing leadership
skills. Books, blogs, seminars, workshops, and retreats are available
for all stages and ages. Retirees are not immune—we recently
discovered that the American Society on Aging has a *Leadership
in Aging* blog. Leadership training is a multibillion-dollar industry
that continues to grow, independent of all economic trends.[1]

Followership, in contrast, is almost completely ignored. We talk
about a call to leadership but never a call to followership. We have
little or no imagination for the gifts or skills of followership. Have
you ever attended a followership training workshop? Imagine a

---

1 "The Leadership Training Market," *Training Industry* (blog), March 28, 2019, https://
trainingindustry.com/.

youth program that marketed itself as "training the next genera-
tion of followers!" Not surprisingly, it seems to be the opposite.
For example, the 2020 season of Girl Scout cookie sales kicked off
with a new fruit-flavored offering, Lemon-Ups, and one of eight
motivational messages stamped and baked into these shortbread
cookies reads: "I AM A LEADER." It is doubtful that "I AM A FOL-
LOWER" was ever considered. Apparently, what's good for cookies
is also good for cars. The new 2019 Volvo S60 is the sports sedan
that rewrites the driving story because it's designed for those who
"Follow No One." This clear aversion to following—both the
word itself and what it stands for—is readily accepted, broadly
promoted, and crosses all generations.

Academic studies of followership have shown some traction
in recent decades, but the amount of literature and the attention
it draws is negligible in comparison to leadership literature. To
put it mildly, it has certainly not lived up to the prediction of
Warren Bennis, who enthusiastically wrote in an introduction
to a 2008 book on followership that within a decade the existing categories of leadership and followership would become
as "dated as bell bottoms and Nehru jackets."[2] His prediction
was based on his sense of the rising appreciation of followership, particularly in the face of what he assumed would be the
erosion of traditional notions of leadership. Yet, a search of
leadership titles on Amazon published since 2010 finds 30,000
books. The same search for followership finds only 70—a ratio
of over 400 to 1. It seems that traditional notions of leadership

---

2   Ronald E. Riggio, Ira Chaleff, and Jean Lipman-Blumen, *The Art of Followership: How
Great Followers Create Great Leaders and Organizations* (Hoboken, NJ: John Wiley &
Sons, 2008), xxvi, ProQuest.

and followership have proven more enduring than bell bottoms and Nehru jackets.

Setting aside the disappointing growth projections for the followership market, it is worth noting that a substantial portion of the followership literature is written with *leaders* in mind. In other words, followers are discussed, but with an eye to making leaders successful. It seems that even books that focus on followership often end up being read through a leadership lens. This is seen, for example, in a leadership blog that reviewed Barbara Kellerman's book *Followership: How Followers Are Creating Change and Changing Leaders*. It is a valuable book, and we were glad to see it garner attention. However, we were surprised to see that the cover of the book had apparently been photoshopped for use as the lead graphic for the blog.[3] The subtitle of Kellerman's book was changed to read "*Good Followers Make the Best Leaders*." Apparently, we can study following as long as it is done for the sake of making leaders. Otherwise, it appears, there would be no point. It is as if followership is a shadow; it is a nothing rather than a something, an absence rather than a presence.

Our book rejects these assumptions about followership. We believe followership is something in its own right, not just the lack of leadership. We believe it is worth studying for its own sake. It has its own set of skills and excellencies; it has its own challenges and rewards. Followership may be a stepping-stone to leadership, and it is certainly an activity that forms character needed for leadership, but it can also be useful in and of itself. It deserves its own Girl Scout cookie. And for Christians, followership is more

---

3   Michael McKinney, "Good Followers Make the Best Leaders," *Leadership Now* (blog), March 14, 2008, https://www.leadershipnow.com/.

foundational to our spiritual lives than leadership. We may move in and out of leadership, but there is never a day when we will not be followers. We are "disciples" of Christ, a term that means followers. We have no higher aspiration than to follow the author and perfecter of our faith.

This book is written with many groups of people in mind. First of all, we write for countless ordinary people faithfully doing the tasks of daily life. You may be a leader in your church or community or you may not. But if you read leadership literature or attend a leadership seminar, you discover that everything you hear is wrapped around a vision for "changing the world" or "making a difference." Very little of what you hear helps you validate and embrace your daily tasks. In fact, quite the opposite—it makes you question the value of your daily life or even disdain it. Tish Harrison Warren expresses this sentiment beautifully as she reflects on her own life, which for many years after college was wrapped up in world-changing pursuits until, after some time, she discovered she had misunderstood the importance of ordinary life. She writes,

> A prominent New Monasticism community house had a sign on the wall that famously read "Everyone wants a revolution. No one wants to do the dishes." My life is really rich in dirty dishes (and diapers) these days and really short in revolutions. I go to a church full of older people who live pretty normal, middle-class lives in nice, middle-class houses. But I have really come to appreciate this community, to see their lifetimes of sturdy faithfulness to Jesus, their commitment to prayer, and the tangible, beautiful generosity that they show those around

them in unnoticed, unimpressive, unmarketable, unrevolutionary ways. And each week, we average sinners and boring saints gather around ordinary bread and wine and Christ himself is there with us.[4]

This book is also written for people with a deeply felt passion and sense of mission. This passion may be a central part of your daily activities or it may be pursued in your discretionary time. Either way, it is something that you clearly see needs to be done. You may not be part of an organization and you may not have anyone who is following your lead, but there is a task that needs to be done, and you are doing it. We have several friends who have a concern like this for children in need. It may be a child from war-torn Africa, it may be a child with a disability, or it may be a child in foster care. These friends have been willing to put their concern into action. They have been foster parents themselves; they have adopted children; they have made room within their families for those from other families. But they have not necessarily started a revolutionary movement or become public advocates for their cause in the community. So do we call our friends "leaders"? We could if we wanted to, but why would we? Most of them are not doing these acts of love because they want to be leaders but because they want to be servants—not servant-leaders, just servants. In this case, they are serving children who need an extensive amount of care. They often lack followers precisely because what they are doing is not an easy job. But their lack of followers doesn't keep them from

---

4 Tish Warren, "Courage in the Ordinary," *The Well* (blog), April 3, 2013, http://the well.intervarsity.org/.

following Jesus's example of letting the little children come to them and loving because he first loved us.

Last, this book is written for people who are part of an organization, church, or business that is pursuing a mission. You may just be playing a small part. Perhaps you have simply been caught up in the passion and mission of others. They are running a soup kitchen because they have a passion for the poor. You just happen to be their friend. You could never see yourself running a soup kitchen, but you can certainly see yourself helping a friend. And you may not have the gift of service, but you can dish out soup with the best of them, so you do it. Every Friday night. And as you do it, the words of Jesus run through your mind, "Inasmuch as you did it to one of the least of these My brethren, you did it to Me" (Matt. 25:40 NKJV). You realize you do it because you have decided to follow Jesus.

So this book is written for disciples—that is, for people who follow. But this book is also written for people who are leaders or, more precisely, for people whose following has put them in a place of leadership. You give direction, make decisions, and cast vision for other people—people who, in the providence of God, have been placed within the scope of your leadership responsibility. And you realize that even as you lead—in fact, especially as you lead—you are still answering your first call, and that is the call to follow Jesus.

We hope that for all these groups of people, this short book will help you appreciate and understand what it means to be a follower. We hope this book will increase the effectiveness of both followers and leaders by promoting common ownership of the vision, deepening our appreciation of one another's contributions, and seeing more clearly where our organizational and vocational tasks fit within our spiritual lives. We hope that it will help you fall in love with following and find that your faithful following becomes a deep well of meaning and a fountain of joy for your life. And we hope that God will use this book to make you contagious—a contagious follower!

# 1

# Of Leading and Following

*Whoever loves his life loses it, and whoever hates his life in*
*this world will keep it for eternal life. If anyone serves me,*
*he must follow me; and where I am, there will my servant*
*be also. If anyone serves me, the Father will honor him.*

JOHN 12:25–26

THERE WILL BE MUCH IN THIS BOOK that challenges common
intuitions about the proper place of leadership in human organizations in general and the Christian life in particular. But we want
to be clear at the outset that our complaints about leadership are
analogous to the complaints that we might make about money.
Money itself is not bad—in fact, quite the opposite. It is a blessing
both to ourselves and to others. It makes possible a whole host of
economic activities that would be impossible in a barter economy.
In so doing, money also makes for economic growth that would be
impossible without it and thereby contributes greatly to prosperity
and human flourishing. Unfortunately, money is also seductive,

deceptive, and dangerous to our souls. It is an instrumental good, meaning that it is good for the sake of other goods, not good in and of itself. But we often pursue money as if its goodness was intrinsic—as if it was to be desired for its own sake. Money is good within bounds: in his prayer found in Proverbs, Agur asks, "give me neither poverty nor riches" (Prov. 30:8). But we often pursue money as if it was a boundless good—as if it was good in any measure and more was always better. Money has a proper place in our wallets, but it often wants to steal a place in our hearts and become an idol, occupying a place that should properly be reserved for God. Money sneaks into our affections, guides our choices, serves as the altar for our most extreme sacrifices, and ultimately tunes its voice to the key of final judgment, whispering, "Well done, thou good and faithful servant." Money is equal parts good and downright scary.

And leadership is like money. Leadership, too, is an instrumental good. It helps get things done. But it is not an intrinsic good—it is not to be pursued for its own sake. We should aspire to serve and love and care for others, and fulfilling those aspirations may require us to lead, but leadership often becomes its own aspiration. We find successful leadership to be satisfying, so we seek to climb the ladder. As with money, we think that if a little bit satisfies, more of it will bring even greater satisfaction. If one promotion is good, two will be better. We lose sight of the needs of others and the flourishing of the whole, which were the goods that originally drew us to leadership, and we focus instead on our own fulfillment. Power and influence become as addictive as wealth and luxury. Leadership can become an idol just as money can—filling our hearts, guiding our choices, demanding our sacrifices, and speaking in the key of final judgment.

Leadership, therefore, should be approached with caution—not because we might fail in our leadership tasks but because leadership can distort our souls, disorder our affections, and draw us to the praise of men rather than the praise of God. Successful leadership can only be sustained by a well-formed soul. In weak souls, it easily becomes a predatory virus that devours its host. One might think that if leadership is so dangerous that we should avoid it altogether but, as we have already seen, it is a needed good. It can be shunned no more than material goods can. And ironically, it is often in accepting leadership tasks that our soul becomes better formed. Virtues demanded in leadership roles are often hard to cultivate in other ways, and becoming fully formed in Christ often demands that we fill leadership roles in one way or another.

Thus, what is needed is a nuanced view of leadership that extolls its benefits even as it warns about its perils. This chapter will take a few steps toward this goal by first identifying some of the common statements about leadership and its importance that we agree with. Then we will turn our attention to some equally common statements about leadership that we believe are either misleading or simply mistaken. The hope is that we can refine our thinking about leadership and generate what communication scholars call "cognitive complexity." We are pushing back against the common perception of the transcendent importance of leadership. Leadership is neither everything nor the only thing; it is just a thing. It has its place, but it is not the highest place and certainly not the only place. In fact, keeping leadership in its place helps keep it healthy. The greatest aid in doing this is to properly value leadership's most intimate companion: followership. Not unlike money and generosity, leadership and followership are born from the same womb and beg to be viewed as beloved siblings. Yet, unfortunately for both followership and generosity, our culture gives them the status of a neglected stepchild relative to their favored siblings—leadership and money. But that is to leap ahead; let's begin by looking more closely at leadership and assessing what we tend to get right about it and what we tend to get wrong.

## Helpful Statements about Leadership

There are several statements about leadership that we fundamentally agree with. Some of them are overstatements and we may feel obliged to moderate them but, nonetheless, they identify real goods of leadership that deserve to be fully appreciated. Here's a short list:

**Leadership is essential to the flourishing of organizations, communities, societies, churches, governments, and businesses.** Every sphere of human endeavor needs good leadership. There is much truth in the famous saying from Alexander the Great, "An army of sheep led by a lion is better than an army of lions led by a sheep."[1] Leadership is essential to organizational effectiveness, and there is really no amount of followership than can make up for its absence. In a similar vein, John Maxwell explains the reason for the rising importance of leadership:

> Why has leadership become so important? Because people are recognizing that becoming a better leader changes lives. Everything rises and falls on leadership. The world becomes a better place when people become better leaders. Developing

---

1   Frederick Thomas Jane, *The British Battle Fleet: Its Inception and Growth Throughout the Centuries to the Present Day* (Boston: Nickerson, 1915), 1:107.

yourself to become the leader you have the potential to be will change everything for you.[2]

This quote needs a bit of nuance—we are not convinced that *everything* rises and falls with leadership or that becoming a leader will change *everything* for you—but it does capture enough truth about the importance of leadership that the hyperbole can be overlooked for the moment.

**Anyone can become a leader, or, at the very least, there is not a single identifiable type of person who can become a leader.** The best leaders are often not the people we would expect. Jim Collins, bestselling author of the book *Good to Great*, illustrates this principle well as he tells the story of what he calls a Level 5 leader:

> In 1971, a seemingly ordinary man named Darwin E. Smith was named chief executive of Kimberly-Clark, a stodgy old paper company whose stock had fallen 36% behind the general market during the previous 20 years. Smith, the company's mild-mannered in-house lawyer, wasn't so sure the board had made the right choice—a feeling that was reinforced when a Kimberly-Clark director pulled him aside and reminded him that he lacked some of the qualifications for the position.[3]

But however mild-mannered his appearance and however weak his qualifications, Smith became a transformative CEO who

---

2 John C. Maxwell, *Developing the Leader Within You 2.0* (Nashville: HarperCollins Leadership, 2018), 1–2.

3 Jim Collins, "Level 5 Leadership: The Triumph of Humility and Fierce Resolve," *Harvard Business Review*, July 1, 2005, https://hbr.org/.

served for two decades and helped make Kimberly-Clark a shocking economic success story. Collins masterfully unpacks Smith's combination of a crystal clear commitment to corporate mission and an iron will to carry that mission no matter the sacrifice. It is a great story, but for present purposes all we really need to note is that the best leaders are sometimes the least likely ones. We don't know ahead of time who will be a great leader, so we are far better off assuming that anyone can lead successfully.

**Leaders need training and equipping—natural skills are not enough.** This fact, combined with the previous observation about the importance of leadership, is sufficient to account for the abundance of leadership training programs. As we will argue, these programs are not without a downside, but nonetheless, leadership is essential to all we do, and therefore doing it better just makes sense. We are certainly not opposed to training and equipping leaders to be more effective.

**Leadership is a gift and calling from God.** God appoints leaders because good leadership is necessary for accomplishing divine purposes and because it blesses those who are led. Part of why we would never encourage Christians to be anti-leadership is that the Bible is not anti-leadership. When God wants to get something done, he calls and appoints a leader to the task. Consider examples like Noah saving a righteous remnant from the flood and Abraham being called out of comfort in Ur of the Chaldees to raise up a people of God's very own. When God saw his people suffering under oppression in the land of Egypt, he called forth Moses to be their liberator. Years later, God sent Samuel to find David and anoint him while he was still tending sheep because he wanted to break the cycles of oppression Israel suffered from its neighboring tribes. The examples are endless. It seems that when a major task is to be accomplished in salvation history, God appoints a human leader to help accomplish the task.

**Leadership should be respected, supported, and encouraged.** Leadership is often a thankless task, so our first calling when it comes to leadership is to be supportive and to help it succeed (Heb. 13:7, 17). Much of the New Testament is written as an encouragement to leaders. It has been recorded for the benefit of all, but it was most commonly written with leadership in mind—guiding leaders and exhorting them to fulfill their calling.

## Harmful Statements about Leadership

Having noted important truths about leadership, let's turn our attention to some statements about leadership that are endorsed by our culture but may not be true. In fact, these statements may even be harmful to individuals and organizations and the missions they pursue.

**Everyone is a leader.** This statement is ubiquitous in leadership literature. A quick internet search will guide you to a host of articles with this phrase in the title. It is usually accompanied by a definition of leadership that plausibly supports this claim. For example, one might define leadership as influence, and since everyone has influence, everyone is therefore a leader. Clearly, part of leadership is influence, and it is presumably true that everyone has some influence on others. But this is like saying everyone is a doctor because we all deal with illness or everyone is a chef because we all prepare food. Defining doctor and chef so loosely simply makes the words meaningless. As Betsy Jordyn notes, "The 'everyone is a leader' myth, which has been blindly accepted as truth, actually waters down the significance and uniqueness of the gift of leadership and keeps people who don't have that gift from finding out what they actually are great at doing."[4]

What, then, is leadership? Admittedly, leadership can be difficult to define. As part of research for his book *The Future Leader*, Jacob Morgan asked more than 140 CEOs from around the world to define leadership. He noted that his interviewees seemed to pause, sensing that leadership was a word that everyone used without really defining. Once the definitions were given, he commented, "From more than 140 people, I didn't receive a single duplicate response."[5]

Though there is truth in what Morgan says about the diversity of leadership definitions, the problem this poses can be easily overstated. As long as we are not seeking a perfect, universal definition of leadership, an ordinary dictionary serves rather well. For example, the *Oxford English Dictionary* entries for "leader" include phrases such as "foremost or most eminent member (of a profession)," "a person of eminent position and influence," and "a person who guides others in action or opinion."[6] Further, a leader is one who "takes the lead in any business, enterprise, or movement and who is 'followed' by disciples or adherents."[7] These definitions serve admirably by making explicit our common intuitions: leaders are people who have followers; leaders are the foremost experts or

4 Betsy Jordyn, "Not Everyone is a Leader," *Purpose to Profits* (blog), January 11, 2017, https://www.betsyjordyn.com/.

5 Jacob Morgan, "What Is Leadership, and Who Is a Leader?" *Chief Learning Officer* (blog), January 6, 2020, https://www.chieflearningofficer.com/.

6 *Oxford English Dictionary*, "Leader," accessed December 7, 2021, http://www.oed.com/.

7 *Oxford English Dictionary*, "Leader."

people of eminent influence; leaders are not just one of the pack, they are people who guide the direction of the pack. If leaders are defined in no small part by the fact that they have followers, then a simple truth emerges: in any given setting, someone has to be the follower, and therefore everyone cannot be the leader.

One might think this is merely a vocabulary problem, a complaint about the way we talk about leadership and nothing more. However, the way we talk has consequences, some of which can be dangerous or destructive both to our souls and the organizations and communities that we are a part of.

We often say that everyone is a leader because we want to be inclusive; leadership is a trophy we want everyone to receive. However, this desire actually hurts and excludes the very people we are trying to include. As we have noted, the plain fact is that in any given setting everyone is *not* a leader; in fact, most members of a group are followers, not leaders. But if we say that everyone is supposed to be a leader, then the word "follower" just becomes shorthand for "failed leader." As a result, being a follower is not defined as a job that one can do well, it is defined as a job that you are failing to do—the job of leading. In this way of thinking, the only way followers really become successful is if they become leaders.

**Everyone should aspire to lead.** Perhaps, one might argue, even if everyone is not a leader at any given time, everyone should aspire to be a leader. If one cannot be a leader in all contexts, at least one can be a leader in some. But why? Why must everyone aspire to leadership? Because leadership is good and following is bad? Because everyone was designed to lead and we should fulfill our design? Because we will never be fulfilled if we are not leaders? There is no reason to believe any of these claims are true.

Beginning with the first claim, there is no reason to accept that leadership is good and followership is bad. They are both necessary. If one is leading, one should be a good leader. If one is following, one should be a good follower. There are good and bad versions of both followers and leaders.

Second, there is no reason to think everyone is designed to lead. When we look at spiritual gifts, leadership (or administration) is one gift among many. It is not a gift given to all. Of course, one could lead even if one lacks the gift, but it is not clear why that would be desirable, much less universally required. It might very well be necessary at times—a fallen world is full of demands that do not always correlate with our gifts or motivations, and we trust that God would give us the grace to rise to the occasion and meet the demands that are placed upon us. That might mean leading in times and places we would rather not be leading in yet are nonetheless called to lead in. But that does not make leadership something that we must aspire to; it simply makes it something we might be called to do by the providential arrangement of the circumstances in our lives.

Third, the idea that we must become leaders in order to find fulfillment and meaning in life seems to be an unlikely claim. Many people do find leadership fulfilling, but that is generally because they have a gift or passion for leadership. Using our gifts and expressing our passions certainly contributes to a flourishing life. As we have noted, however, everyone is not gifted as a leader and everyone does not have a passion to lead. Some serve under the leadership of others and find themselves quite happy and fulfilled. They rejoice in the success of the organization that they are a part of. They rejoice in the contributions that they make to the organization.

They may particularly rejoice in making contributions that others cannot—in feeling needed, essential, even irreplaceable. But they can experience all these joys without being christened as "leaders." So why should contentment in following be viewed as a character flaw that needs to be corrected? It is difficult to make that case.

In short, none of the reasons suggested above actually support the claim that everyone should desire to be a leader. It is true enough that no one should decide ahead of time that they will refuse to be a leader. The mere fact that some people don't feel like leadership material is certainly no guarantee that they are not going to be called to lead. As previously mentioned, some of the best leaders are people who initially seemed unlikely or unqualified—not just business leaders like Darwin Smith but also biblical leaders like Moses and Gideon and Jeremiah. However, the willingness to lead when called upon and everyone having an obligation to lead are two very different things.

**If you are not leading, you are missing out or being irresponsible.** A further consequence of our cultural tendency to make everyone a leader is that those who do not lead are told that they are leaving their potential undeveloped. As John Maxwell states, "You have influence in this world, but realizing your potential as a leader is your responsibility. If you put effort into developing yourself as a leader, you have the potential to influence more people and to do so in more significant ways."[8] It would seem those who do not become leaders are burying their talent in the ground—a strategy that ended rather badly for the servant in Jesus's parable. This contributes to feelings of guilt and frustration

8  Maxwell, *Developing the Leader Within You 2.0*, 5.

for those who are not leading. It may also lead to feelings of injustice when a person is not given their supposed chance to lead. Finally, it may result in people working for leaders who are not particularly gifted or motivated to lead but feel obliged to because they would hate to be accused of following the example of the unfaithful steward and burying their talent in the ground.

**Leadership is an essential mark of Christian maturity.** When we universalize the call to leadership and combine it with stories like the parable of the talents, it is hard for leadership *not* to be viewed as a fundamental mark of Christian maturity. But in reality, though biblical leaders are called to be mature, every mature person is not called to lead. Leadership is not a fruit of the Spirit, and it is the fruit of the Spirit that characterizes Christian maturity. One can be loving, joyful, peaceful, patient, kind, gentle, and self-controlled without being a leader. Go back and reread this list—are these the qualities that we uniquely associate with leaders? Certainly not. We might like it when our leaders are this way but these are not the defining characteristics of leadership, nor are they characteristics that are uniquely associated with leaders. In fact, our normal stereotypes seem to associate these qualities more closely to followership than leadership.

**Leadership is the goal we aim for.** Making leadership a proper expectation for each and every person turns leadership into the equivalent of the North Star. The North Star is an easily visible fixed point by which we navigate. It orients us, and by keeping it in sight we know where we are and if we are going in the right direction. Much of our education, sociology, politics, and government navigate by the star of leadership. Those working in these areas ask who and how many are leaders. They are preoccupied with paths to leadership and train and equip people to travel down these paths. To be clear, we (Rick and Joanne) don't think the path to leadership is a bad path, and we certainly don't think the path to leadership should be barred to any person ahead of time, especially not based on race, class, or gender. Dismantling such obstructions is a noble cause and will greatly improve our institutions. Making leadership our sole point of navigation, however, is dangerous.

I (Rick) learned a lot about the proper place of leadership from my father. He spent his vocational life as a research scientist. He was exceptionally good at it and seemed to thoroughly enjoy his work. However, he never really climbed the corporate ladder. He never became the head of his research group or division. And I never spent a lot of time thinking about this as I was growing up. Dad seemed happy enough with his work, so why would I think about it? After I graduated from college, I spent some time working in a research lab myself as a means of paying for seminary. As I watched how the lab worked, I realized that the leader of the research lab spent very little time actually doing laboratory research. In fact, in three years of working there, I don't recall actually seeing him working in the lab at all. However, he was constantly raising funds, serving on committees, networking with influential leaders, and dealing with institutional management issues. His days were not spent in laboratories but in meeting rooms, banquet halls, and boardrooms. He was a very effective laboratory director. And I realized that my dad would have *hated* doing that job! He loved doing things hands-on—tinkering with things on his workbench, inventing things from scratch. My laboratory director, on the other hand, loved seeing all those things get done, not doing them himself. He and my dad had a very different set of motivations. And

I'm grateful that my dad was wise enough to navigate by what he loved and what he was good at, not by the siren call of leadership.

Similarly, we need to be very careful of what we are viewing out our windshield as opposed to what we can see out our side windows. Christians in particular are called to keep the love of God and the love of neighbor squarely in front of them, visible through their windshield. These loves are not the same thing as leadership. As we pursue love of God and love of neighbor, leadership opportunities may very well come along, but they approach from the side. They join in on a journey that is not headed to the land of leadership but to the land of love and service.

## Conclusion

We hope that we have made it clear that we are not opposed to leadership. In fact, we are actually great fans of it. We just want to make sure we keep leadership in its proper place, and that place is not every place. In fact, we wish leadership advocates would spend a little more time identifying the proper place of leadership for individuals and organizations and a little less time trying to sell leadership to each and every person. We wish for such a change not because we want to devalue leadership but precisely because we respect and value it—we should avoid bleaching it out and making it apply to every person at every place and time. And we should also release people from the relentless obligation to lead. Leadership is a calling, leadership is a gift, and leadership is a responsibility, but it is not the only calling, it is not the only gift, and it is not the only responsibility. In fact, one of the most important insights we would offer in this book is that despite many myths to the contrary, followership is every bit as much of a calling, gift, and responsibility as leadership is.

## 2

# Mistaken Beliefs about Followership

*When followers follow effectively they help ensure
that the leader leads effectively and the organization
advances towards its goal; when they don't, that usually
results in the leader and the organization failing.*

MICHAEL CONNOLLY JR.

FOLLOWERSHIP, LIKE LEADERSHIP, is prone to misunder-
standing. Unlike leadership, however, followership has few (if
any) positive perceptions in contemporary culture. In the 1990s,
David Berg conducted several training seminars on leadership
and followership and reported that participants used words like
"sheep," "passive," "obedient," "lemming," and "serf" to describe
followers—hardly an attractive description.[1] Similarly, a recent
academic literature survey says that followership stereotypes

---

1   David N. Berg, *The Psychodynamics of Leadership* (Madison, CT: Psychosocial Press,
    1998), 29, EBSCO.

view followers as recipients or moderators of leaders' influence (Shamir, 2007) who dutifully carry out the orders, directives, and whims of the leader, without resistance or initiative (Kelley, 1988). Not surprisingly, the resultant focus has been nearly exclusively on leaders, and the vast history of research on leadership can be viewed as the study of leaders and "subordinates."[2]

We believe these offer fairly accurate descriptions of followership stereotypes, but they are far wide of the mark when it comes to a vision of what followership really is. We also believe this (mis)perception of followership is harmful and dangerous to organizations, leaders, and followers alike. When our organizations expect followers to be weak, easily led, and mindlessly dependent on leadership, they will get exactly that. When leaders expect these qualities in those who follow them, they will lead as if they alone understand the mission of the organization and the way it can be achieved. And when followers conceive of themselves in this fashion, the low expectations make them see themselves as "just followers" or "mere followers," which in turn leads to passive detachment from the mission of the organizations they serve. Such detachment saps energy and creativity from the organization and also drains the jobs we do of the meaning we might otherwise find in them. It is important, therefore, that we rethink and correct our stereotypes of followership.

### Followership Defined

Before we consider mistaken beliefs about followership, we should offer a simple definition and a few clarifications of what this defi-

2    Mary Uhl-Bien et al., "Followership Theory: A Review and Research Agenda," *Leadership Quarterly* 25, no. 1 (February 2014): 84, https://doi.org/8ps.

nition does and doesn't mean. First, let's consider efforts to define followership from academic literature. One source summarizes,

> Following behaviors represent a willingness to defer to another in some way. DeRue and Ashford (2010) describe this as granting a leader identity to another and claiming a follower identity for oneself. Uhl-Bien and Pillai (2007) refer to it as some form of deference to a leader: "if leadership involves actively influencing others, then followership involves allowing oneself to be influenced" (p. 196). Shamir (2007) argues that following is so important to leadership that it negates the construct of shared leadership altogether: "leadership exists only when an individual (sometimes a pair or a small group) exerts disproportionate non-coercive influence on others" (p. xviii).[3]

Clearly, a defining characteristic of followership in all these descriptions is a posture of deference to a leader. But this isn't enough. Almost all studies of followership also identify other characteristics like engagement and mission ownership. For example, one scholar writes that "what distinguishes an effective from an ineffective follower is enthusiastic, intelligent, and self-reliant participation—without star billing—in the pursuit of an organizational goal."[4] Any full definition of followership, then, should include (1) deference (otherwise it doesn't have the core conceptual distinction between leaders and followers), (2) zeal and engagement (otherwise a person is not actively following, they are

---

3  Uhl-Bien et al., "Followership Theory," 83.
4  Robert E. Kelley, "In Praise of Followers," *Harvard Business Review* 66, no. 6 (December 1988): 143.

simply being led or dragged along), and (3) mission ownership (otherwise following is for the sake of following itself, not for the sake of successfully doing a worthy task).

Some might object to the idea of deference because it sounds like it reinforces the passive stereotype, but the other two aspects of this definition help to avoid this error. Engagement and mission ownership require a deference that is freely and actively chosen. There is no room in this definition for coerced following or passive following. The follower is leaning into and pressing forward with the task at hand—a task that they fully own and are personally committed to. It should also be noted that the same literature that identifies deference as part of followership frequently includes lengthy discussions of leadership and followership as a joint venture and ongoing relational process, even describing leadership as being "co-produced" by leaders and followers.[5] Thus the deference we are considering here is not the passive, sheeplike obedience that is disdained and mocked in our stereotypes.

Overall, the definition we have just drawn from the academic literature is largely compatible with Christian thought about followership, though we would add an important qualification. Any particular role of following is subordinate to our highest call of following: we follow Christ (deference) through the power of the Spirit and with all our heart, mind, soul, and strength (engagement

---

5  B. Shamir, "From Passive Recipients to Active Co-Producers: Followers' Roles in the Leadership Process," in *Follower–Centered Perspectives on Leadership: A Tribute to the Memory of James R. Meindl* (Greenwich, CT: Information Age, 2007); Uhl-Bien et al., "Followership Theory: A Review and Research Agenda"; Gail T. Fairhurst and Mary Uhl-Bien, "Organizational Discourse Analysis (ODA): Examining Leadership as a Relational Process," *The Leadership Quarterly* 23, no. 6 (December 2012): 1043–62, https://doi.org/gfzswn.

and zeal) in order to glorify God and build his kingdom (mission ownership). So for those who follow Christ, all of life's roles and responsibilities are part of such following. It is also essential that we understand that the pervasively negative attitude we have toward deference and subordination runs afoul of biblical attitudes toward followership. Obviously, we follow Christ himself, but we also follow human leaders he has put in authority over us, including both secular rulers (Rom. 13:1) and spiritual overseers (1 Thess. 5:12–13). Our first biblical identity is one of followership—and if that notion is distasteful to us, it is likely that we have some work to do in transforming our own heart attitudes.

Having now defined followership, we are prepared not only to leave behind simplistic stereotypes but also to think more deeply about some of our more subtle and hidden misperceptions.

### Followership Exists for the Sake of Leadership

Though followership involves deference to leadership, such followers ought not think of their lives as revolving around the leader. However, this is not always easy in a world where organizational charts are usually just leadership charts that almost intentionally ignore the co-productive nature of leadership and followership and poorly reflect the necessity for good followers. Similar problems are found in many authors who study, research, and write on followership due to the fact that they approach followership from the perspective of organizational leadership or outcomes.[6] They

---

6  Laurent Lapierre, *Followership: What Is It and Why Do People Follow?* ed. Melissa K. Carsten (United Kingdom: Emerald Publishing, 2014), 13–14, 19–20; Robert Kelley, "Rethinking Followership," in *The Art of Followership* (Hoboken, NJ: John Wiley & Sons, 2008); Thomas A. Atchison, *Followership: A Practical Guide to Aligning Leaders*

thus focus on questions like how a leader can gain and manage a more numerous and responsive group of followers.

When followership is leader-centric, the mission of an institution, company, organization, or church recedes into the background. Leader-centric followers seek to please the leader and often end up losing themselves in their attempts to be the person they think the leader wants them to be. They may lose sight of the original mission and end up focusing on the rewards and benefits that come from pleasing the leader such as career advancement, pay raises, or simply the satisfaction of being included in the inner circle of the organization. Such following leads to jockeying for position, unjustifiably protecting or flattering the leader, and drawing one's self-worth from the leader. The unintended consequence of these behaviors is that followers lose contact with their own unique purpose and sense of calling. They find themselves lacking in personal growth and suffering from muddled answers to the question, "Who am I?" Their own ethical standards may be subordinated, suppressed, or simply disregarded because of their desire to please their leader. They really only know themselves through the eyes of their leader.

Instead of being leader-centric, good followership needs to be mission-centric. The follower's first commitment is to a mission, not a leader. Convinced of an institution's mission and committed to strive collaboratively toward achieving it, one then accepts the role of a follower within an organization that includes deference to a particular leader. The key point, however, is that this move is

*and Followers* (Chicago, IL: Health Administration, 2004), 199, 205; John Antonakis and David V. Day, *The Nature of Leadership* (London: Sage, 2017), 332ff; Barbara Kellerman, *Followership: How Followers Are Creating Change and Changing Leaders* (Boston, MA: Harvard Business, 2008).

made because followers, leaders, and the organization as a whole share a commitment to a common mission.[7] Mission-centric followership validates our Spirit-given giftings and fosters personal responsibility because one senses not only an organizational commitment to a particular mission but also a divine calling to that mission. In other words, the reason one joins an organization is that one sees its mission as a legitimate expression of God's calling on one's own life. When the organizational mission is attached to one's divine calling, two important things happen. First, one's service to an organization becomes more intrinsically significant; it gains meaning because it advances God's work in the world. Second, and perhaps paradoxically, it is easier to keep one's missional commitment in its proper place. It does not stand alone but rather within a set of divine callings to family, church, neighbor, and personal holiness. Followership, so conceived, exists for thriving and sustainable relationships with God and others in community. Of course, your colleagues and co-workers will be impacted, but that impact spreads well beyond the walls of any cubicle, office, or business complex. The influence and appeal of one's followership reaches across the globe, street, hall, conference call, and dinner table.

### Followership Is an Unworthy Goal

Another mistaken stereotype is that followership is a temporary necessity that must be endured or, better yet, circumvented. One's

---

7　Chaleff has convincingly argued for the importance of leaders and followers being mutually committed to the mission of the organization. See Ira Chaleff, *The Courageous Follower: Standing Up To and For Our Leaders* (Oakland, CA: Berrett-Koehler Publishers, 2009), ProQuest.

*real* identity is as a leader, and one must merely suffer through a season of followership as a means to the end of leadership. The tasks of a follower are simply resumé building, done only for the prospect of being rewarded with leadership opportunities, roles, and titles. But such aspirations circumvent the true significance of followership and often foster naïve arrogance that detracts from the goal of growing in Christlikeness. Ultimately, dismissive attitudes toward following compromise one's credibility in an organization, community, or church.

The commitment to follow well is a worthy calling in and of itself, a fact that is made very clear in Scripture. A disciple (learner) of God is most fundamentally a follower—in this case, a follower of Jesus. Followers of Jesus have far-reaching impact and influence, and they do not have to become leaders in order to have such impact. As followers, we simply join in what God is doing in the world; our lives are written into his story. Finding one's position as a leader is not nearly as important as understanding one's place as a follower within God's kingdom. The calling to serve as a follower does not rely on drawing attention to oneself but to the God who calls us to represent him in spheres of influence as his ambassadors as well as witnesses of his Spirit residing within.

### Following Is Passive and Requires Few Gifts or Abilities

At the outset of this chapter, we identified the stereotype of followers as sheep or lemmings that lack the capacity to think for themselves or the confidence to lead others. It is worth examining this sort of thinking more carefully. There is an unstated assumption in this line of thought that followers and leaders are two different types of people. Leaders have authority, charisma, power, influence, and significance, so they set the ground rules and make important decisions. Followers don't. Followers, in effect, are defined by what they are not: they are not leaders.[8] It is assumed that they are not qualified or equipped to contribute significantly to a group, project, organization, or church. They are people who rubberstamp the ideas of those with greater creativity and influence.

Fortunately, thinking of followers as a particular (and deficient) kind of person is beginning to change, not only because of biblical correctives such as those we have already mentioned but also because of research done within the context of business and management. As early as the 1970s, E. P. Hollander and his colleagues were studying the way people viewed followership. They realized there were significant defects in the traditional view of a follower as a particular kind of person, discovering that

> it is commonly assumed that a cleavage exists between those who lead and those who follow, and that being a follower is not being a leader. . . . Only some members of a group have "leadership qualities" . . . and stand out as "leaders." . . . Followers are treated essentially as "nonleaders," which is a relatively passive residual category.[9]

Hollander's point is that it is a mistake to assume that leaders are leaders because they possess certain essential leadership qualities

---

8  Melissa K. Carsten, Peter Harms, and Mary Uhl-Bien, "Exploring Historical Perspectives of Followership: The Need for an Expanded View of Followers and the Follower Role," in *Followership: What Is It and Why Do People Follow?* (London: Emerald Publishing, 2014), 13.

9  Susan D. Baker, "Followership: The Theoretical Foundation of a Contemporary Construct," *Journal of Leadership & Organizational Studies* 14, no. 1 (August 2007): 53.

or that followers lack these qualities. He argues that "leader" and "follower" are better understood as roles and processes, and that these roles and processes should not be confused with the people filling them. Robert Kelley, one of the founders of modern followership studies, develops this point more fully in his seminal article, "In Praise of Followers." He writes,

> If a person has initiative, self-control, commitment, talent, honesty, credibility, and courage, we say, "Here is a leader!" By definition, a follower cannot exhibit the qualities of leadership. It violates our stereotype. But our stereotype is ungenerous and wrong. Followership is not a person but a role, and what distinguishes followers from leaders is not intelligence or character but the role they play. As I pointed out at the beginning of this article, effective followers and effective leaders are often the same people playing different parts at different hours of the day.[10]

Thus, Kelley offers a twofold corrective to the traditional stereotype of the follower. First, just like Hollander, he points out that followership should be viewed as a role not a person. Second, he notes that most people fill both roles, not just at different times in their lives but often at different times during a single day! So the idea that followers and leaders are fundamentally different types of people is simply mistaken.

Having made this point, Kelley goes on to describe people who are effective in the follower role. They are people who

10  Kelley, "In Praise of Followers," 146.

have the vision to see both the forest and the trees, the social capacity to work well with others, the strength of character to flourish without heroic status, the moral and psychological balance to pursue personal and corporate goals at no cost to either, and, above all, the desire to participate in a team effort for the accomplishment of some greater common purpose.[11]

Far from the faceless masses of the subservient, good followers exhibit a remarkably high level of aptitude and depth of character—and these qualities are all the more admirable for the fact that they often go unrecognized. The competence and work ethic exhibited by followers underscore both their knowledge of an organization and their vital gifts and abilities. Good followers constitute the essential means for success in any organization, company, or church.

### Follower Images Are Unattractive and Repugnant

If the first thing that comes to mind when people think of followers is a serf or a lemming, it is easy to understand why they find followership unattractive or downright repugnant. But perhaps they are just using the wrong imagery. Perhaps using biblical imagery of followership would make it more attractive. Unfortunately, biblical imagery does not fare much better. The next two sections of this chapter will look at biblical imagery for followers and try to understand why it strikes us as negative.

One of the most pervasive metaphors for followers in the Bible is actually sheep. We tend to despise the notion of being

---

11 Kelley, "In Praise of Followers," 147.

a sheep—being a sheep is just as bad as being a lemming or a serf. However, there is simply no denying the fact that this is a metaphor the Bible uses (and uses frequently) to describe people who faithfully follow after Jesus. More troubling still is the fact that biblical imagery usually invokes aspects of being a sheep that are exactly the sorts of things that trouble us. Sheep are not just prone to follow, they need to follow because they are in some sense dependent on the shepherd. In biblical teaching, sheep consistently need a shepherd; sheep without a shepherd is always a negative image that forebodes disaster for the sheep.

But this does not exhaust the way the Bible describes sheep. Though sheep need a shepherd and are meant to follow, biblical metaphors do not picture sheep as mindless followers. In fact, it is quite the opposite. John 10:5 makes it clear that the sheep follow because they recognize the voice of the shepherd, and if they hear a stranger, they will not follow but rather flee from him. So the sheep are not stupid or mindless: they will follow a voice they recognize as the good shepherd's but refuse to follow a stranger. John goes on to note that the false voices calling to the sheep are not simply strangers (like the voices of shepherds who care for other flocks) but rather robbers and thieves—people who are intentionally trying to deceive and exploit the sheep. So the good sheep, as depicted in John 10, are what we might call "deception proof" (or, at the very least, "deception resistant"). They just plain refuse to listen to these deceptive voices (John 10:8). They are aware that one voice is trying to lead them to their own demise and destruction and the other voice is leading them to abundant life (John 10:10). So, though good sheep still need to be led, they are also very discerning about the voice they will follow.

And on the theme of good sheep, it should also be noted that there is such a thing as a bad sheep. This is implied in John 10 but much more fully developed in another extensive biblical passage about sheep and shepherds: Ezekiel 34. Here, Ezekiel compares the nation of Israel to a flock of sheep, and that flock includes sheep who push and shove and bite and batter the other sheep. Clearly, sheep can be either good or bad. And shepherds, likewise, can be good or bad, depending on whether or not they police the misbehaving sheep. Ezekiel is speaking to a nation that is in exile because of its failure to keep God's covenant, and he portrays this as a failure of both leadership and followership, both shepherds and sheep. Furthermore, toward the end of Ezekiel 34, David is explicitly referred to as a shepherd of Israel (v. 23). Yet, this same David, the prince and shepherd of Israel, also refers to himself as a sheep in Psalm 23. David is the perfect example of the point made earlier: "follower" is a role, not a description of a particular kind of person, and therefore the same person is often found serving in both leadership and followership roles—both sheep and shepherd.

## *Follower, Servant,* and *Slave* Are Oppressive Terms

Most people don't like being called a follower, much less a servant or slave. We hear these terms as repressive and associate them with racism in particular and, more generally, with worthlessness, insignificance, and misery. But these associations come from our own cultural context and we should not assume that the same associations are found in the biblical context. We hear these words so differently than the authors of the Bible did that we have to make a substantial and intentional effort to understand what they meant in their original context. And if we don't make this effort, we will never grasp the closely related concept of following.

The New Testament Epistles offer some helpful guidance in reconceptualizing servanthood. In his letter to the Corinthian believers, Paul expounds on what it means to be a servant, slave, and follower. The Greco-Roman culture highly esteemed status, authority, and privilege, but Paul flips the thinking of his readers, arguing that the apostles should not be viewed as powerful people but rather as servants or slaves. He goes so far as to use the language of ownership, saying that the apostles are the ones who belong to the Corinthians (1 Cor. 3:21–23).[12] As a servant, one is "tasked by a master, who is their source of growth (3:6), the object of their service, and to whom they are responsible."[13] Thus, Paul sees himself as a servant whose worth and identity come from God and are attached to his appointed service, not from his own status or acheivements. In 1 Corinthians 3:5, Paul asks *what* Paul is and *what* Apollos is instead of *who* Paul is or *who* Apollos is. He is drawing the reader's attention to the role and task of the servants rather than the servants themselves.[14] God and what he is doing is the object of attention, not Paul or Apollos. Thus, Paul does not advocate for merely having a servant attitude but actually being a servant in the fullest sense of the word.

These passages make clear that even established leaders of the church were perceived as followers, both in terms of the way they saw themselves in relation to Jesus and the way they wanted to be

12  Michelle Lee-Barnewall, *Neither Complementarian Nor Egalitarian: A Kingdom Corrective to the Evangelical Gender Debate* (Grand Rapids, MI: Baker Academic, 2016), 108.

13  Lee-Barnewall, *Neither Complementarian Nor Egalitarian*, 109.

14  Andrew D. Clarke, *Secular and Christian Leadership in Corinth: A Socio-Historical and Exegetical Study of 1 Corinthians 1–6* (Milton Keynes: Paternoster, 2006), 119–20.

seen by their correspondents. In the church, leaders were considered followers, servants, and even bondslaves. The connotations of these words were negative, demeaning, and harsh, even in the New Testament world. Nonetheless, Paul intentionally chose to use such words because he wanted to subvert and transform the Corinthians' view of servanthood. The simple fact is that Paul was so emphatic about his self-understanding—as a follower of Christ, a slave of Christ, before all else—that he boldly, even joyfully, took on labels that his culture would have viewed as degrading and dishonoring. Paul knew the Master and what he was like and fully depended on God to accomplish his purposes. He wanted these same attitudes to develop in those who followed him.

The relationship between servant and master is aptly illustrated by Peregrin Took, affectionately known as Pippin, in J. R. R. Tolkien's fantasy novel *The Lord of the Rings*. Pippin, a lowly hobbit, comes to Denethor, the mighty Steward of the High King, with the tragic news of the death of Denethor's favorite son, a powerful leader and warrior. He doesn't know what else to say after giving him the news of how his son died protecting him, so he pledges his fealty to Denethor as a lifelong bondslave. Consider both the words of Pippin's pledge to Denethor and Denethor's response:

Pippin: Here do I swear fealty and service to Gondor, and to the Lord and Steward of the realm, to speak and to be silent, to do and to let be, to come and to go, in need or plenty, in peace or war, in living or dying, from this hour henceforth, until my lord release me, or death take me, or the world end. So I say, Peregrin son of Paladin of the Shire of the Halflings.

Denethor:   And this do I hear, Denethor son of Ecthelion, Lord of Gondor, Steward of the High King, and I will not forget it, nor fail to reward that which is given: fealty with love, valour with honor, oath-breaking with vengeance.[15]

Clearly, the pledge of servanthood is a life-altering pledge. It is a big deal—taken seriously by both Pippin and Denethor. In fact, Denethor gives Pippin a reciprocal promise: to reward fealty and valor with love and honor but to punish oath breaking with vengeance. This image offers a helpful upgrade to our thinking, which diminishes the meaning of servanthood to near triviality. Pippin and Denethor offer a good example of the sense of urgency and importance that the apostles brought to following Christ, as well as the seriousness with which Christ took their service. If one's central life goal is self-expression or personal preference satisfaction, the kind of following that Pippin pledges is doubtless an undesirable goal. But for those who understand what it means to serve a worthy lord, servanthood is a profoundly meaningful life commitment.

## Leadership Requires Training but Followership Does Not

As we write this in the summer of 2021, over 4,000 books on leadership have been published this year, an average of 22 books per day. Our educational institutions in the United States offer 469 organizational leadership degree programs, a number that does not include educational or international leadership programs.

---

15  J. R. R. Tolkien, *The Return of the King* (New York: Ballantine Books, 1965), 29–30.

Predictably, the numbers for followership are almost exactly the opposite. Eight books on followership have been published in 2021, averaging 1 per month, not 22 per day. There are no degree programs in followership. Whether these numbers indicate a lack of demand, a lack of theoretical or theological imagination, or simply a latent cultural expectation, it is clear that even if one wanted to train followers, it would be a lonely task.

It is likely that the underlying reason that followership training seems so counterintuitive is that we are still held captive by the stereotype of followers as sheep or lemmings. Surely it does not take any training to follow the lemming in front of you off a cliff. But as we have pointed out in this chapter, this is a false stereotype—or perhaps better put, a stereotype of a bad follower rather than a good one. Could you imagine corporations making decisions about leadership training based on an ideal of bad leadership? Who needs training to shout at people and make bad decisions! Let us all agree that doing something badly doesn't require training. The point is that both leadership and followership, when aimed at a good ideal, are activities that are important and demanding, and not many of us are fully equipped to do them well.

We have cited Robert Kelley previously, and for good reason. He writes with a robust imagination for the value of effective followership and an obvious concern for the danger of ineffective followership. He advocates for training that cultivates the essential qualities of a good follower: independence, critical thinking, and self-management. These followers know they have something valuable to contribute and have an internal passion to do their job well. Such followers place a premium on building their own competence. Kelley explains that good followers often set their own performance standards and that those standards are higher than what the work environment requires; they are also drawn to continuing education because it helps them achieve the level of excellence they have set for themselves.[16]

If Kelley is right, then we should assume not only that followers can be trained but also that they want to be trained. Further, Kelley reminds his readers that not everyone is an effective follower. He identifies "less effective followers" as people who are not interested in training: "The only education they acquire is force-fed. . . . Their competence deteriorates unless some leader gives them parental care and attention."[17] Fair enough. The point, then, is to clarify the difference between effective and ineffective followers and then use this information to create institutional expectations against ineffective followership and provide adequate training and rewards for effective followership.

Another reason for having followership training is that it goes hand in hand with leadership training. Kellerman asserts that excluding followership from the leadership curriculum is both theoretically indefensible and practically irresponsible. She adds that good training needs to include how to collaborate and compromise, serve and support good leaders, challenge bad leaders, and speak truth to power.[18] What is learned as a follower informs, maintains, and sustains good leadership. In

16  Kelley, "In Praise of Followers," 145.
17  Kelley, "In Praise of Followers," 145.
18  Barbara Kellerman, *The End of Leadership* (New York: HarperCollins, 2012), 194.

the marketplace, personal and professional development is a must for followers as well as leaders.[19] Failure to examine the purpose and practice of following leaves one less equipped for meaningful conversations, relationships, and engagement with others and self.

In addition to the qualities that Kelley and Kellerman suggest, we would add certain qualities of heart that are necessary for biblical followership. High on this list are godly attributes like integrity, humility, love, compassion, commitment, and perseverance. These qualities are best viewed as essential outcomes of Christian formation—they are the fruit of practicing spiritual disciplines or soul rhythms. They are certainly necessary for effective followers, but for Christians they are also essential aspects of a Christlike character. In this regard, followership training is actually spiritual formation, a notion we will take up more fully in chapters 6 and 7.

It should be clear by now that the popular stereotype of followers as sheep and lemmings is grossly mistaken. Indeed, it is not only mistaken by biblical standards but also by the standards of many influential secular thinkers. The simple fact that it is mistaken, however, does not keep a stereotype from being prevalent and influential. It would be good to do some self-reflection about your personal conception of followership. Look at the table below and determine when your own intuitions and assumptions about followership are more in line with the common stereotypes or with biblical teaching.

---

19 Allen Hamlin, *Embracing Followership: How To Thrive In a Leader-Centric Culture* (Bellingham: Kirkdale, 2016), 63–64; Peter G. Northouse, *Leadership: Theory and Practice*, 3rd ed. (Thousand Oaks: Sage, 2004), 317.

| Followership Stereotype | Biblical Followership |
| --- | --- |
| I think of myself as a second-string worker just waiting for my chance at a starting job. | I fully engage in my present role as a follower and find it demands my best efforts. |
| I am concerned how my leader views me because much of my purpose and worth are derived from this perception. | I consistently work as if God's eye is upon me and I find great purpose and worth in doing things in a way that pleases him. |
| I find my character is often tested or compromised as I attempt to move up the leadership ladder. | I consistently guide my choices and make my decisions in light of my Christian convictions and core values. |
| I spend a lot of time looking for something better to come along. | I spend a lot of time looking for new ways to express my organization's purposes and mission. |
| My prayer life focuses on asking God for a fast-track promotion or leadership role. | My prayer life focuses on opportunities to serve others and learn the lessons God has for me. |
| I am tempted to criticize others (privately or openly), including both my fellow workers and my leaders. | I intentionally honor others both privately and publicly, looking for opportunities to highlight everyone who contributes to the mission of the organization. |
| I am prone to manipulate circumstances and conversations to gain recognition from others. | I am content with letting others take credit. |
| I see my current job as meaningless or having little impact except as a stepping-stone. | I see my current job as an opportunity to serve, advance God's kingdom, and help other people around me to flourish. |
| I am disengaged from the decision process since I don't have the final say. | I am engaged in decision making whenever I have direct or indirect opportunities to influence, even if I don't have the final say. |
| I often find myself envying others when they receive praise and accolades. | I can joyfully celebrate the success of others. |

Where do you see yourself as you look through these two columns? Are there any issues that made you feel uncomfortable? Are there any things that you sense God might want you to change? If you find yourself resonating with the second column, you are well on your way toward faithful followership. However, if we're honest with ourselves, most of us have also struggled with the attitudes and behaviors of poor followership described in the first column. But an anemic view of followership makes it impossible to aspire to be a good follower (why aspire to do a meaningless job well?) and negatively affects the very relationships ordained to help us thrive.

## Conclusion

We need to cultivate a vision of followership that demands the very best of our gifts and abilities yet at the same time includes real respect and deference to our leaders. We need a vision for followership that demands our intellect, engages our emotions, and exercises our wills—because otherwise, part of us is still sitting on the sidelines. We need to be engaged with others as a committed team or, to use the biblical metaphor, as a single body where each of us is committed to the whole and therefore concerned for each part and also subordinate to the head. It is not an easy or comfortable view of followership, and we will find little or nothing in contemporary culture that fosters this sort of thinking. Therefore, it is extremely important that we turn our attention to the biblical vision of followership.

3

# A Kingdom of Followers

*Christ came into the world with the purpose of
saving, not instructing it . . . he came to be the
pattern, to leave footprints for the person who
would join him, who would become a follower.*

SØREN KIERKEGAARD, *PROVOCATIONS*

TO HEAR MANY CHRISTIANS TALK TODAY, one would think that
leadership was the hallmark of discipleship and that Jesus promised
to create a kingdom of leaders. But this is to turn the Scriptures on
their head. The hallmark of the disciple is following; the citizenship
in God's kingdom that Jesus offers is reserved for those who choose
to *follow* him. Some followers may be called to lead in particular
times and places. Even for those who receive a call to lead, however,
it is subsequent and subordinate to their call to follow.

Why do we make this claim? Because of overwhelming biblical
evidence. Let's take a quick look at what the Bible says about the
person of Christ himself, the descriptions of discipleship in the

Gospels, and the teaching about discipleship in the rest of the New Testament.

## Jesus As a Follower

The New Testament leaves no doubt as to the deity of Christ. He is the Alpha and the Omega, the beginning and the end. He is the creator of all things in heaven and on earth, both visible and invisible. He calms storms, casts out demons, raises the dead, forgives sin, and presents himself as the only way to eternal life. He has the keys of death and Hades. He is the ruler of the kings of this earth and all authority in heaven and earth is subordinate to him. I'm sure one could extend the list of majestic descriptions of Jesus to fill this entire book. So perhaps it is unsurprising that we forget that Jesus was also a follower.

Indeed, it is a worthwhile project to draw a second portrait of Jesus from the New Testament writings—different from the one we've just drawn—that highlights the manifold representations of his followership. To aid the process, let's first call to mind some of the commonplace differences between a leader and a follower. The leader is the sender; the follower is the sent one. The leader's will is asserted; the follower implements it. The leader writes the message; the follower delivers it. The leader is the exemplar, and followers are only such to the extent they follow the given example. The leader gives the commands; the follower obeys them or passes them along to others. The leader has the authority, and the follower only has whatever authority was delegated by the leader.

With this in mind, if you think that the Gospels will portray Jesus as a leader, you're in for a surprise—when Jesus describes himself and his ministry, he consistently uses the language of following. His human incarnation is the incarnation of a follower. A brief survey of John, the Gospel in which Jesus is most prone to offer self-descriptions, exemplifies this point well.

In John 5:19, Jesus describes himself as a follower who does nothing of his own accord but only what he sees the Father doing. The Father is his exemplar; Jesus only does what the Father does. In 5:36 he points out that his works testify that he has been sent. In 6:38 he makes it clear that he is not acting on his own will but rather subordinates his will to the one who sent him. Then, in 7:16 and 8:26 we discover that his teaching is not his own but comes from his sender and that he declares only what he has heard from him. Likewise, his actions are not done on his own authority (8:28) and his comings and goings are appointed by someone else (8:42). Though he has the authority to lay down and take up his own life, he does this in response to a charge received from the Father (10:18). The sheep who know and follow his voice are not really his sheep but rather a gift received from the Father (10:29). Jesus clearly states that he is not giving commands but rather delivering them on behalf of the Father (12:49). He is an ambassador for the Father, therefore receiving him is actually to receive the Father (13:20). In the upper room, Jesus reminds the disciples that his words are not spoken on his own authority (14:10) and that he lives as one who obeys commands (14:31). He models love to them because he is following the example he has seen in the Father (15:9), and he models obedience because it is the key to abiding in the Father's love, both for himself and for the disciples (15:10). At every point in this mosaic of images, Jesus is playing the role of a follower rather than a leader. Does it look like the Gospel of John was written so that we can lead like Jesus led or so we can follow like Jesus followed? Clearly, it is the latter.

The incarnate Christ is absolutely relentless in teaching us that he is imitating the example, obeying the commands, passing on the teaching, following the timing, submitting to the will, accepting the charge, and receiving the gift of his Father. Jesus is a follower. He is not just a follower in some halfway sense, in the sense of feigned humility, or by virtue of an overinflated definition of following. Rather, he is a full-throated follower who is not merely performing the tasks of following but embracing followership with the flaming zeal of a man sold out to and swallowed up in a divine calling. Jesus had an extremely robust vision of the significance of following.

It is worth adding that Jesus didn't engage in following as a preliminary training activity—following was not a spiritual discipline like fasting or meditation. His fundamental self-presentation to his disciples was as a follower at any and every moment. It wasn't one of his many tasks, it was his defining task. And, importantly for us, his guiding passion appears to be that his disciples imitate him on exactly this point. Our master is a follower, so we are to become followers as well.

Taken together, these teachings of Jesus make a strong case for the value of good following. Yet, despite the secure biblical foundation for this picture of Jesus's followership, such notions often fall on deaf ears, both today and in the first century. James and John were disciples of Christ from the beginning and were constantly immersed in the call to follow. They still, however, grabbed their mother and came to Jesus to beg the favor of sitting in positions of authority—sitting at his left and right hand. There are so many ways Jesus might have put them in their place. But instead of a blunt put-down, he simply reminded them that he himself was a follower and thus was the wrong person to ask for a leadership position. As he put it, "to sit at my right hand or my left is not mine to grant" (Mark 10:40). Then he went on to remind them that he himself, their master, was actually a servant. Biblical scholar Leon Morris summarizes the point of this passage well:

> The feetwashing that John records was a striking illustration of Jesus's readiness to take the place of one who serves, even though he held the supreme place. . . . Jesus is not saying that if his followers wish to rise to great heights in the church they must first prove themselves in a lowly place. He is saying that faithful service in a lowly place is itself true greatness.[1]

Those who want to be faithful disciples do not need a position of authority but rather a heart of service—indeed, a heart for the slave-like service of washing feet. It is worth noting that the other disciples were upset by James and John's request, which is hardly surprising. But this shows that they had completely misunderstood Jesus as well. As Morris notes, greatness is found at the foot of the table. If the call of Jesus is a call to be a servant, having James and John move up to Jesus's right and left hand would have meant that the privileged seats of servanthood located further down the table were still available for the other disciples. They should have been pleased instead of upset!

---

1    Leon Morris, *Luke: An Introduction and Commentary* (Downers Grove, IL: Intervarsity, 2015), 326.

These examples from John's Gospel are obviously accounts of the teachings and practices of the incarnate Christ. They are not meant to repudiate or invalidate descriptions of Christ found in the Epistles or the book of Revelation, which often refer to the preincarnate Christ, Christ at the right hand of the Father, or an eschatological vision of Christ in the age that is yet to come. The Gospels simply focus on Jesus in his humanity. It is noteworthy, however, that Paul describes the incarnate Christ in Philippians 2. Here, Paul identifies Christ's heart of humility and servanthood, which serves as the wellspring of the incarnation. Gerald Hawthorne is right to note that we do not imitate Christ by quitting our heavenly glory but rather by striving to "emulate the attitude and actions of servanthood that marked the character and conduct of the pre-existent Christ."[2]

Further, Jesus as a model of following is not just a New Testament conception of the Messiah, as many of the most striking prophetic passages of the Old Testament offer the vision of the servant of Yahweh. There is some scholarly debate concerning the subject of this image. Some view it as a clear reference to the Messiah and take the fulfillment of these passages to be found in the life of Christ, while others have argued that it refers to Israel in a corporate sense—a remnant community living out covenant faithfulness in spite of persecution and hardship. Either way, it is striking to note the description of this figure. First, and most obviously, he is described as a servant—not a king or a priest or even a prophet (Isa. 42:1–4; 49:1–6; 50:4–9; 52:13–53:12). His

---

2 Gerald F. Hawthorne, "The Imitation of Christ: Discipleship in Philippians," in *Patterns of Discipleship in the New Testament*, by Richard N. Longenecker (Grand Rapids, MI: Wm. B. Eerdmans Publishing, 1996), 169.

demeanor is equally striking. He is gentle and doesn't raise his voice. He won't even extinguish a faintly burning wick or break a bruised reed. His message is not his own but rather is taught to him—language that reminds us of Jesus's own teaching coming from the one who sent him. His task is to bear a burden—in this case, a burden of affliction and crushing oppression that came about because of the transgressions and iniquities of the people. His lifestyle is not a desirable one; it leaves him despised, rejected, and unesteemed. Clearly, this figure is accomplishing God's purpose of setting the world right. It should startle us, then, that he is given the title of servant of Yahweh rather than leader of Yahweh.

## Jesus and His Call to Discipleship

Given Jesus's self-understanding as a follower, it is hardly surprising that when he calls his disciples, he issues a call to follow. If Jesus is a follower then obviously his disciples will be followers as well. But the vividness and strength of a disciple's call to follow merits more careful attention.

### *The Urgent Call to Follow*

An immediate response to Jesus's call is one of the most clearly repeated patterns in the Gospel records. Jesus turns to someone and commands, "Follow me!" and they respond by promptly leaving behind their friends, family, nets, and tax-collecting booths (Matt. 4:23–25). It is as if they were being commanded to flee a burning building. Those who hesitate to follow offer various excuses—caring for a dying father or saying farewell to those who are at home (Luke 9:59–61)—and they are deemed unworthy of being disciples. Following is so urgently important that it demands an immediate response, and, at times, Jesus describes delayed following as tantamount to failure to follow.

## *The Demanding Call to Follow*

The call to follow is not only urgent, it is also demanding. Jesus could not be more transparent about the cost of following. The cost is not just the friends and family and nets that are abandoned on the spot. Jesus seems to relish in clarifying the extremity of the cost. Biblical scholar R. T. France puts it well:

> Those who followed Jesus did so with their eyes open. Because of the division which Jesus provokes within families (Matt 10:34–36), true discipleship may bring a conflict of loyalties, and in that case, following Jesus must take precedence over the natural love of family. . . . The Christian may even have to leave his family (Matt 19:29). . . . Worse still, the disciple will find that in following Jesus he must take his cross.[3]

Indeed, Jesus repeatedly associated the call to follow with the call to take up one's cross (Matt. 10:38; 16:24; Mark 8:34; Luke 9:23; 14:27). There was little ambiguity in what this meant after Jesus's crucifixion. And it is not only crucifixion but death in general that seems to him to be a fitting description of the life of the follower (John 12:25–26). His disciples clearly got this message—on some occasions they boldly proclaimed their willingness to pay the price of following even unto death (Mark 14:31; John

3  R. T. France, *The Gospel According to Matthew: An Introduction and Commentary* (Grand Rapids, MI: Wm. B. Eerdmans Publishing, 1985), 189.

11:16; 13:37), and at other times they acknowledged the price but wondered aloud what the payoff would be (Matt. 19:27–30). In all cases, it was clear that following was not a small matter but one of gravest import, highest cost, and most esteemed reward.

## *The Personal Call to Follow*

It is striking how little content is included in the call of Christ to his disciples. Usually, it is a simple command: "Follow me!" Sometimes he offers a hint of the mission: "Follow me, and I will make you fishers of men" (Matt. 4:19). This phrase, however, offers little information about a new mission. Instead, it issues a call of absolute abandonment of their current activities: "Leave the boats and nets behind and follow me!" In doing this, they are not just swapping fishing for fish with fishing for men but with following Jesus. They are appointed to be with him, walk with him, and learn from him. It is a call to personal attachment to Christ.

Jesus tends to give no reasons for following him. If a prospective disciple doubts or hesitates, Jesus just moves on. The person is forced to choose between the call to follow Christ and all other obligations. In the Gospel narratives, following Jesus is not the sort of decision that is squeezed out of a long chain of systematic reasoning—it is the sort of decision one is compelled to make by Christ himself. His very person is the plausibility structure of the choice to follow. It is made reasonable simply by seeing and hearing Jesus himself. Once your heart is won to Christ, it is lost to all else.

In John 10, answering this compelling call to follow Christ is pictured as sheep recognizing and responding to the voice of their shepherd. They seem to have an ear for his voice and an inability to recognize anyone else's (John 10:4–5, 8, 14–16). It is not like the shepherd offers a good reason—he doesn't shout, "Hey, I found some really green grass and some nice, still water!" He simply calls and the sheep come after him. They implicitly trust that he will lead them to green grass, still waters, and safe refuge, but the call is based on the relationship itself, not the likely rewards. The shepherd calls, and I rise and follow.

Reflecting on the way Jesus issues his call to follow led me (Rick) to a disturbing self-realization. I had spent years in pastoral ministry encouraging people to participate in the various ministries in our church. When I was asking for participants, I usually offered a general call from the pulpit or in written communication. When I was asking someone to be a leader, I always met with that person face-to-face. I wanted to convey a personal interest in their decision and also a sense of urgency and importance. There is a logic to this since taking on a leadership role usually requires more detailed information that is best given in person. Looking back, however, I cannot help but think that part of why I did this was because I was failing to appreciate the urgent importance of the call to follow.

## Imitation and Following in the Epistles

Moving from the Gospels to the Epistles, the New Testament vision for followership emerges in even fuller relief. To see this clearly, we must first realize there is a change in vocabulary between the Gospels and the Epistles—Jesus consistently refers to his disciples as followers, while the writers of the Epistles tend to favor the language of imitation. The concepts remain very similar; though followers of Christ are now referred to as imitators of Christ, the essential descriptions of the Christian life remain firmly entrenched in the followership motif rather than the leadership motif.

## The Language of Following

One of the striking features of New Testament vocabulary is the lack of leadership terms and the abundance of followership terms. Andrew Clarke, a New Testament scholar at the University of Aberdeen, notes that many words for "leader" were available in Hellenistic Greek, two of which are extremely common in the Septuagint. But, Clarke continues, New Testament vocabulary is quite different. He explains that

> although both of these words also occur in the New Testament, they are not only much less widely spread . . . they are also much less frequent. Furthermore, where they do occur, they are largely in reference to the Jewish synagogue or nation, the imperial rulers of the day, or demonic powers. The general designation "leader" is for the most part either not used in reference to the early Christian communities or its nature is explicitly redefined or qualified.[4]

This lack of leadership terms is partly due to the focus on following and other closely related ideas. As we have noted, Jesus uses "followers" again and again to describe his disciples. And as we work through the rest of the New Testament, we discover many similar words: imitation, example, model, and pattern. In fact, words like these are used almost thirty times in the Epistles to describe disciples or discipleship. They are not only abundant in Paul's writing but also spread throughout all the other Epistles as well.[5]

4  Andrew D. Clarke, *A Pauline Theology of Church Leadership* (London: A&C Black, 2007), 1–2.
5  Clarke, *A Pauline Theology of Church Leadership*, 173.

A striking vision of discipleship begins to emerge when you read these letters. Paul puts it very succinctly in 1 Corinthians 11:1 when he exhorts the Corinthians to imitate him as he imitates Christ. When Paul embarked on his mission to Thessalonica, he says he was intentionally offering himself as a model and he commends them for imitating him and his companions and, in so doing, becoming an imitator of Christ (1 Thess. 1:5–6). A more graphic image is found in 2 Thessalonians 3:9 (as well as 1 Thessalonians 2:8) where Paul uses the language of self-giving sacrifice, stating that he and his companions gave themselves as "an example to imitate." Other New Testament writers also advocate for following and imitating using similar language (Heb. 6:12; 13:7; 1 Pet. 5:3).

Overall, the New Testament conceives of discipleship as a chain of followership much more than a chain of leadership. The general hallmark of the faithful Christian is being a faithful follower. Followers are also leaders in the sense that they inspire others by their good example, though their example is only good to the extent that they are faithfully following. An easy way to visualize what is happening is to imagine a game of follow the leader with an ever-increasing line of followers. At some point the line becomes so long that the next follower can no longer see the leader at all, so they just follow the person in front of them, trusting that that person is faithfully following the leader. The next to last person in line has become a leader for the last person in line, but those who become a leader in this sense are probably not thinking of themselves as leaders at all. In fact, they may not even know that someone is watching them instead of the real leader.

This almost unintentional leadership is explicitly encouraged by Paul. He commends the Thessalonians because they imitated him and his companions, but then he notes that the Thessalonians themselves became a model and that their testimony inspired other followers throughout Macedonia and Achaia (1 Thess. 1:8–9), a fact that the Thessalonians would have been unaware of until Paul told them. In other cases, Paul points out that he may no longer be present but exhorts the church to identify those who are faithfully following his instructions and imitate them (Phil. 3:17). Paul may have a special apostolic calling, but he is not unique in his role as a model for others; he expects all those in the church to take up this mantle. Thus, believers model Christ to one another both individually and corporately. Entire churches imitate one another—believers in Macedonia and Achaia are imitating the Thessalonians, and the Thessalonians are imitating the churches in Judea (1 Thess. 2:14). The legacy of Paul's missionary journey is a mammoth game of follow the leader that stretches across the Mediterranean world and produces a chain of followership insistently focused on the person of Christ himself—no matter how many intermediaries lie between him and the follower.

Of course, included in this vast chain are countless people who are also serving in leadership roles. This is seen partly in the use of student and teacher images that are similar to those of imitating and following. For example, Paul, who has taught Timothy, asks him to teach other faithful men, who will then teach others (2 Tim. 2:2). Congregations are asked to consider the outcome of the way of life of the leaders who taught them God's word and to imitate them (Heb. 13:7). Thus, there is clearly an expectation that there will be recognized elders and leaders in congregations, and the Pastoral Epistles give clear instruction as to the character and competence that is expected of these leaders. So the prevalence and priority of followership by no means precludes the presence of leadership in the New Testament Epistles.

However, though it is true that no adequate account of New Testament discipleship can ignore leadership, it is equally true that New Testament leadership did not map easily onto surrounding Greco-Roman models of leadership. As has already been mentioned, shunning leadership terms and multiplying followership terms is the first clue to this tension. Furthermore, Paul is intentionally distancing himself not only from those who use power-laden leadership terms but also from those like the Sophists, who use the language of imitation but in a way that puts the teacher at the top of a hierarchy. Paul's vision of imitation is seeking the advantage of the many rather than his own.[6] His desire is not to interpose himself between Christ and the Corinthians but rather for them to see Christ more clearly through his example and ultimately to become models of Christ themselves. In summary, Witherington notes that "whatever sort of hierarchy Paul presupposes, it entails an inverted pyramid where leaders are enslaved, belong to the community, and must serve it from below."[7] This vision of leadership reinforces the priority of followership in one's self-understanding, even if one is filling a leadership position. This inverted and contrarian vision of leadership also emerges from the elements of the life of Christ that Paul chooses to model. He does not ask his readers to imitate the strong visionary leadership of Jesus or his harsh treatment of the Pharisees and money changers. Rather, he wants to imitate Jesus's humble, self-sacrificing commitment to the interest of others, even

6   Ben Witherington, *Conflict and Community in Corinth: A Socio-Rhetorical Commentary on 1 and 2 Corinthians* (Grand Rapids, MI: Wm. B. Eerdmans Publishing, 1995), 145.
7   Witherington, *Conflict and Community in Corinth*, 145.

at the expense of his own interest, to the point of losing his very life. Jesus practiced this (Phil. 2:1–10), Paul aspired to it (Phil. 3:8–10), and his readers are called to imitate it as well.

Finally, Paul did not measure successful apostolic leadership by acclaim and glory. When forced to legitimize his apostolic calling to a skeptical audience, as he was in 2 Corinthians 11:7–33, the evidence he gave was his refusal to take money, exercise privilege, demand his rights, or make use of his status or prestige. He also called to mind his persecution, suffering, imprisonments, and forced flights in the dark of night. One could hardly imagine validating hallmarks that were more contrary to the prevailing culture's vision of leadership. Undoubtedly, they are equally counterintuitive today.

## Followership and the Lordship of Christ

The final piece of New Testament teaching we will consider is the lordship of Christ. His lordship demands our followership. As Peter says in stunned response to God's calling of the Gentiles, he is Lord of all (Acts 10:36). He is Lord of all people—both Jew and Gentile. He is Lord of heaven and Lord of earth. He is Lord of every ruler, principality, and human authority. He is Lord of creation and creatures alike. He is Lord of the future and the past; Lord of our churches, our communities, and our families. He is the Lord of each individual heart. There is nothing we see, nothing we do, nothing we hope for, nothing we dread, nothing we desire, and nothing we shun that does not rise or fall by his voice. He is indeed Lord of all.

For this reason, we look first to him. We see him through our windshield and our prevailing culture only through the side windows. Our personal preferences and cultural attachments account for little or nothing. Why? Because Jesus is not just *the* Lord but *our* Lord. His lordship is personal to us. If his will is clearly expressed in Scripture, we do it, no matter our culture's preferences or practices or predilections. If he demands something that is contrary to the habits of our family of origin or the inclinations of our favorite group, political party, or academic school of thought, we must choose allegiance to him rather than attachment to our group. Notice that in all of these cases, the reason we take a different path is not because we are leaders but because we are followers—followers of Christ. It is not because we think for ourselves but because we try to think like Jesus. It is not because we can't please everyone so we please ourselves but rather because we seek to please Jesus above ourselves. To view Jesus as Lord of all, and to choose to follow him without looking back, means that we are not so much independent thinkers but rather Christ-dependent thinkers. We see our world and our life projects through the lens of following Christ.

The understanding of leadership advocated in the bestselling books of our day is almost exactly the opposite. All too often, leadership is a self-expressive project. Popular leadership thought is all about scripting your own life, charting your own course, and creating your own reality. It is extremely self-centered in the exact meaning of the phrase—the project of leadership is centered on oneself. Consider these affirmations from a leadership website that one is encouraged to repeat to oneself several times each day:

1. I am enough.
2. I let go of all that no longer serves me.
3. I am brave, fearless, bold and strong.

4. I attract only good things into my life.
5. I have the freedom and power to create the life I desire.[8]

These affirmations are found in *A Beginner's Guide To Mindfully Manifesting Personal And Professional Goals*. The idea of mindfulness is drawn from Buddhist teaching, which has been made popular by recent psychological literature. Unfortunately, the ideas don't seem that much different in popular Christian literature. Here's a sampling of aspirations from Laurie Beth Jones's bestselling book, *Jesus CEO*:

"I shape my own destiny."

"What I believe, I become. What I believe, I can do."

"I proudly say I AM, knowing clearly my strengths and God-given talents. I repeat my strengths to myself often, knowing my words are my wardrobe."

"I release others so that I myself can fly."[9]

The brute fact is that both of these popularized visions of leadership, whether Buddhist or "Christian," are at odds with the lordship of Christ. They are self-expressive and devoid of any sense of discipleship as self-abandonment. These descriptions of

---

8 *A Beginner's Guide to Mindfully Manifesting Personal and Professional Goals* (Millennium Systems International, 2018), 5, https://www.millenniumsi.com/.

9 Laurie Beth Jones, *Jesus, CEO: Using Ancient Wisdom for Visionary Leadership* (New York: Hyperion, 1995), 295.

leadership are simply incompatible with the complete lack of self-absorption that the lordship of Christ demands of us. They are far, far removed from the attitude of Paul who recites his accomplishments at length and then dismisses them completely, saying that he counts them as dung because of the all-surpassing worth of knowing Christ Jesus his Lord. He lets go of all he has done, all that he has desired, all to which he has aspired. He leaves these things behind to pursue the upward call of God in Christ Jesus (Phil. 3:14). If we are to recapture a biblical understanding of followership, we must begin with Paul's example and recenter ourselves on Christ as Lord—the Lord who we follow in place of our own personal desires, aspirations, and accomplishments.

## Conclusion

The main point we have argued in this chapter is not the insignificance of leaders but the overwhelming importance and ubiquity of followers in Scripture. Most particularly, we want following to be viewed as an aspiration and a calling—something worthy of our highest efforts. Followership is also something we will never grow out and never aspire to grow out of. Our faithfulness in following will allow others to follow us, and in that sense, we will often lead. But this sort of leading could never be viewed as graduation from or a replacement for following. We never reach a point in the Christian life where we can afford to take our eyes off the high calling of followership because Jesus is building a kingdom of followers. The great aspiration of the Christian life is to hear the words, "well done, thou good and faithful servant" (Matt. 25:21 KJV) not "well done, thou good and faithful leader."

4

# A Crisis of Followership

*There is a vast literature of failure of leadership—*
*Who will write the essay on the individual*
*and collective failures of followers?*

JOHN GARDNER, *THE HEART OF THE MATTER*

WE LIVE IN TROUBLED TIMES. Polarization and anger prevail in both the public square and in our churches. Church splits and civil wars are increasingly becoming a tangible fear instead of a vague anxiety. Those in positions of power often exhibit striking moral flaws—and at times they even flaunt those flaws. Tragically, this seems to be as true of our pastors as our politicians. Our pundits bemoan these developments as a crisis of leadership. But are leaders to blame?

We often assume that bad leaders lead good people astray. When church and country lose their way, it is because bad leaders fooled or corrupted good followers. No doubt this happens at times. It is, however, extremely misguided to assume that the quality of followers plays no role in the quality of the leaders over them. Indeed, as we shall see shortly, leadership correlates with followership, and even more ominously, leaders are often providentially appointed as a judgment on followers. In other words, there are times when God sends weak or evil leaders as a means of judging people who are straying from his covenant, dishonoring his name, or abandoning their mission.

On January 6, 2021, while we were writing this chapter, the Capitol Building was stormed by protestors. Like countless other Americans, we watched in horror as the events unfolded. We witnessed one policeman bludgeoned by a fire extinguisher and another being beaten with a flagpole. Elected officials were ushered from their chambers while their staff huddled under tables, fearing for their lives. It was an appalling scene.

A common refrain of journalists and politicians in response to these events was to distance the rioters from the American people as a whole. As Congressman Adam Kinzinger put it, "we (Americans) are not what we are seeing today."[1] Likewise, then President-elect Biden said that the actions of the mob did not reflect America. But John Stonestreet, president of the Colson Center for Christian Worldview, saw things differently. He lamented,

I wish [Biden] were correct. But he wasn't. We are not a moral nation. We are lawless. We are not a nation that cultivates the kinds of families able to produce good citizens. Our institutions cannot be trusted to tell us the truth or advance the good. Our

---

1    "Bill Hemmer Reports, Fox News, January 6, 2021, 12:00pm–1:00pm PST," *Internet Archive*, 00:00-00:02, http://archive.org/.

leaders think and live as if wrong means are justified by preferred ends. Our churches tickle ears and indulge narcissism. Our schools build frameworks of thinking that are not only wrong, but foster confusion and division.[2]

Tom Nichols, professor at the U.S. Naval War College, expresses similar sentiments. Looking back at the events of January 6, 2021, he points his finger at what he believes to be the greatest threat to democracy in the United States: we the people. He confesses,

This is hard to say and it was hard to write. It would have been easier to find other culprits and unite with my fellow Americans in a tribal and bracing hatred of globalization, or China, or immigration, all of which are real issues that require wiser policies. But democracy is not unwinding because of container ships or communists. It is on the ropes because of our own choices. We, ourselves, have become unwilling to engage in civic life at even the most basic level of regular voting. We, ourselves, have embraced consumerism that demands ever better and ever cheaper products no matter what the cost to our own economy. We, ourselves, have chosen to be solitary viewers of television and social media, and then to express ourselves in public only with performative and childish rage.[3]

---

2 John Stonestreet, "What If What We Saw Yesterday at the Capitol Is Us?" *BreakPoint*, January 27, 2021, https://www.breakpoint.org/.

3 Tom Nichols, "Trump Is Not Ruining Democracy, We Are. And It's Been Anguishing to Confront," *USA Today*, August 19, 2021, https://www.usatoday.com/.

We believe Stonestreet and Nichols are right. America is not a moral nation. These are hard and unwelcome words to say, but they are true. Certainly, leaders have a share in the blame, but no more than the broad base of citizens who make up the tattered fabric of our society. Our families, churches, and schools share in the responsibility for failing to produce a nation of good citizens. In fact, the lion's share of the blame lies not with the leaders of our country but the citizens. This was not first and foremost a crisis of leadership but of followership.

## Leaders, Followers, and the American Nation

Why do we make this claim? First, America was never designed to flourish because of the virtue of its leadership. In fact, the country was founded by people who were deeply suspicious of leaders. They knew and valued the importance of good leadership, but they also filled our founding documents with checks and balances against abuses of power. The teeth of those checks and balances resided in the citizenry as a whole. Leadership was necessary, but it was also to be held accountable by followership. Branches of government had boundaries that limited abuse and excess, but the ultimate check and balance was the vote of the people. Elected officials answered directly to the people in each election. Judges were appointed rather than elected, but those appointments were made by elected officials who could be voted in or out partly on the basis of the sorts of judges they appointed. Ultimately, America's accountability structures depend on the moral health of the citizenry. The design of our government was doomed to fail if the citizens were not virtuous.

John Adams stated it this way: "Public virtue cannot exist in a Nation without private Virtue, and public Virtue is the only Foundation of Republics."[4] Elsewhere, he is even more adamant: "We have no government armed with power capable of contending with human passions unbridled by morality and religion. . . . Our Constitution was made only for a moral and religious people. It is wholly inadequate to the government of any other."[5] Adams's sentiments were shared by a host of other founders, such as those listed below:

Benjamin Franklin: "Only a virtuous people are capable of freedom."

James Madison: "To suppose that any form of government will secure liberty or happiness without any virtue in the people, is a chimerical [imaginary] idea."

Thomas Jefferson: "No government can continue good but under the control of the people; and . . . their minds are to be informed by education what is right and what wrong; to be encouraged in habits of virtue and to be deterred from those of vice."

Samuel Adams: "Neither the wisest constitution nor the wisest laws will secure the liberty and happiness of a people whose

---

4   A. Koch and W. Peden, eds., *The Selected Writings of John and John Quincy Adams* (New York: Knopf, 1946), 57.
5   Charles Francis Adams, ed., *The Works of John Adams, Second President of the United States* (Boston, MA: Little, Brown, 1854), 9:229.

manners are universally corrupt. He therefore is the truest friend of the liberty of his country who tries most to promote its virtue."[6]

We quote these architects of our political institutions at length to convey how clearly they saw the importance of followership for the integrity of our system of government and the flourishing of our nation. In their mind, bad leadership was to be expected if the citizenry (followership) was not exhibiting moral virtue in their public dealings and political expectations.

## Leaders, Followers, and the Church

Similar principles are found in Scripture. Leadership failure is intimately connected to followership failure. Bad shepherds can destroy the flock, but flocks can go bad as well. Ezekiel 34 offers a clear example of both. The chapter begins with a judgment on shepherds who exploit the flock for their own purposes, but it ends with an equally strong condemnation of members of the flock who push, shove, and trample the pasture and pollute the water. Flocks can go bad from above or below—and, of course, the failure of one amplifies the failure of the other. But Christian theology doesn't stop here.

### *Leaders as a Judgment on Followers*

In a lengthy discussion of human magistrates and the providence of God, John Calvin notes that "those who rule for the public benefit are true patterns and evidences of this beneficence of [God's];

6   J. David Gowdy, "No Liberty Without Virtue," *The Washington, Jefferson & Madison Institute* (blog), April 3, 2011, http://wjmi.blogspot.com/.

that they who rule unjustly and incompetently have been *raised up by him to punish the wickedness of the people.*"[7] In his commentary on Romans 13:3–4, which states that human authorities are appointed by God to reward good and punish evil, Calvin further explains that this is God's normal intention for magistrates and their people. However, he also states that those who hold power often depart from this ideal. Though this seems like a failure in the leader, Calvin argues that since "a wicked prince is the Lord's scourge to punish the sins of the people, let us remember, that it happens *through our fault* that this excellent blessing of God is turned into a curse."[8] Clearly, Calvin sees a strong causal connection between the character of followers and the quality of leaders God appoints over them.

Further biblical illustrations of this principle are not hard to find. In Exodus 32:24, Aaron made a golden calf while Moses was meeting with God on Mount Sinai, but he did so in response to the people who demanded it (Ex. 32:24). He could hardly be accused of leading the people astray—they were straying long before Aaron got his interim leadership appointment. Most of the language of Exodus 32 attaches the responsibility for the sin to the people as a whole (vv. 1, 7, 9, 11, 22, 30) and only to a lesser degree to Aaron (vv. 21, 25). Indeed, one might say that his leadership opportunity was providentially arranged to give full display to the rebelliousness of the people as a whole (Deut. 8:2). A similar story can be told of Samuel, who gave Israel a king not because he wanted to but because the people demanded it

---

7 John Calvin, *Institutes of the Christian Religion*, trans. Henry Beveridge (Grand Rapids, MI: Eerdmans, 1989), 670; emphasis added.

8 Calvin, *Institutes*, 670; emphasis added.

of him. God commanded him to grant their wish, but he also commanded Samuel to give the people a warning that getting what they wanted would be its own judgment for rejecting God as their king (1 Sam. 8:4–22). Habakkuk also clearly saw the moral failure of Judah and pleaded for God's intervention. God confirmed Israel's moral failure and assured Habakkuk that he would respond but, unfortunately, his response was to send the Babylonians as conquerors. Habakkuk was shocked and appalled but ultimately stated, "O Lord, you have ordained them as a judgment" (Hab. 1:12). Time and again, by request or by conquest, God uses leadership as a judgment on followership.

The biggest lesson to draw from all of this is that the quality and nature of leadership can never be separated from the quality and nature of followership. Followership and leadership are joined at the hip. Both leaders and followers affect each other and both are responsible for the well-being of the community. It is disingenuous, deceitful, and dangerous to ignore the responsibility that followers have for the failures of their leaders. On the contrary, the normal expectation is that leaders embody the virtue and character of their followership. Our leader's moral failings commonly mirror our own.

Our inability to see a connection between followers and leaders is one more example of the theme of this book: we lack any positive vision for followership. If followership by nature is passive and disengaged, one cannot really be judged for doing it well or poorly. It isn't really an action at all. But if followership is a substantial thing—if it requires a vision of a goal and an iron commitment to a mission, if it demands virtue and courage, if it was the aspiration of the incarnate Christ, if it is the vision of Christian discipleship that permeates the New Testament, if followers are to test the teachings of their leaders and hold false teachers accountable, and if faithful followers put their hands to the plough and never look back—then surely following can be done well or poorly, or even not at all. And it would certainly make sense for God to judge his people and hold them accountable for their failures as followers as well as commend and reward them for their successes.

## Followers and the American Church

The examples we have considered thus far have focused mainly on what might be called civic or political leadership, whether in the ancient biblical context or in the contemporary American context. What we have seen thus far should confirm John Stonestreet's accusation that we are overly quick to blame our leaders and mistakenly excuse American citizens as a whole. But it is appropriate to also ask if the church is doing any better than the nation. Are American Christians faithfully discharging the duties of followers and are they holding leaders accountable to faithfully discharge their duties as well? Unfortunately, the answer seems to be no.

Recent years have seen an abundance of scandals involving Christian leaders of the highest profile: Ravi Zacharias, Bill Hybels, Carl Lentz, Jerry Falwell Jr., James MacDonald, and Mark Driscoll, to name a few. The scandals vary from sexual misconduct to financial corruption to abusive leadership. And of course, the list of offenders and offenses could be greatly extended. For our present concerns, however, the important thing is not the fact that various evangelical leaders have engaged in egregious behaviors that have brought shame to the body of Christ. In a fallen world, we must assume that leaders will not be exempt from moral failure. Rather, our concern is the stunning lack of urgency that congregations and organizations seem to feel about matters of basic accountability. The cavalier approach to accountability structures, which must be owned and implemented by the followership, go a long way in explaining the shame that leadership failures have brought on the body of Christ.

Christian author and journalist Andy Crouch recently reflected on a week in which "three separate cases in my immediate circles, a person with significant power at the top of an organization, each one a subject of flattering major media exposure during their career, was confronted with allegations of sexual misconduct and related misdeeds."[9] Though he was not sure if the accusations were true, he realized that there had been institutional failures at least as profound as the leadership failures. He explained,

> The most damning facts in the disheartening emails and news reports that came across my desk this week are not about the alleged actions of certain leaders . . . *but the uncertain and partial reactions of the systems around those leaders.* When boards are beholden to founders; when elders allow it to be publicly said that "no one person can replace" a senior pastor; when information systems can yield the number of emails exchanged between a senior leader and a given person but somehow the content is not recoverable—none of this means that any malfeasance has been committed. But it does mean

9 Andy Crouch, "It's Time to Reckon with Celebrity Power," *The Gospel Coalition*, March 24, 2018, https://www.thegospelcoalition.org/.

that the sheer gravitational pull of those charismatic figures has nullified the institution's ability to protect itself, and indeed its leader, from both legitimate and falsified allegations of misconduct.[10]

Crouch's point is that institutions must hold followers and leaders accountable to one another and to God himself. Responsibility for misconduct cannot be confined to the failed leaders.

Ed Stetzer, executive director of the Wheaton College Billy Graham Center, offers a helpful summary of this entire discussion:

> The past half decade has offered near daily examples of people co-opting the gospel for sinful ends. Racism, nationalism, sexism, and host of other sins have found purchase within the evangelical movement in both overt and subtle expressions. . . . Many have been able to dismiss these examples as outliers that did not truly represent the evangelical movement. We have long since exhausted this excuse. As evangelicals, we have to stop saying this isn't who we are. This is who we are; these are our besetting sins. However, this isn't who we have to be.[11]

In the memorable words of the cartoon character Pogo, "We have met the enemy and he is us!"[12] It is time we honestly face

---

10  Crouch, "It's Time to Reckon with Celebrity Power"; emphasis added.

11  Ed Stetzer, "Evangelicals Face a Reckoning: Donald Trump and the Future of Our Faith," *USA Today*, January 10, 2021, https://www.usatoday.com/.

12  Walt Kelly, *Pogo*, April 22, 1971, ink and blue pencil on paper, 39.5 × 34.5cm, Pogo Collection, Billy Ireland Cartoon Library and Museum, Columbus, https://library.osu.edu/.

our failings and recommit ourselves to the arduous task of faithful following by reforming our souls, renewing our institutions, and reinventing the relationship between leaders and followers.

## Toward More Faithful Followership

Thus far, this chapter has argued that the ills facing our country and the evangelical church are not primarily a matter of leadership but of followership, or, at the very least, that followership is much more responsible for our problems than we commonly think it is. This may sound fine and good, but it is natural to wonder what this actually looks like in practice. For example, what can I, as an ordinary church member, do when my pastor is exercising his authority in an abusive fashion? I may see it and believe it is wrong, but since I'm not on the elder board, the pastor doesn't report to me. Similarly, what can I do if my political party is losing its bearings but I don't feel any better about the other party? I'm not a professional politician, nor do I have time to add grassroots political activism to my schedule. What can a follower really do to make a difference?

First, let's be clear that we are not arguing that leaders do not matter at all but rather that we have acted like they are all that matters. We somehow expect that good leadership will fall upon us like manna from heaven. We rarely, if ever, stop to think that the most immediate way to improve our leadership is to improve our followership. We need followers with the wisdom to identify good leaders and the courage to reject or remove bad leaders. So the first thing that followers can do is work to improve leadership through the many and various means that are available to them. Secondly, followers can develop certain habits of thought and patterns of conduct that strengthen an organization. Thus, we conclude this chapter by considering what these habits and actions might look like.

## See Something, Say Something

Followers need to develop a habit of speaking up. When we are followers, we are often on the front lines and see a lot of things that those in leadership may miss. We are also often the first people to see misbehavior and sinful conduct that both our leaders and peers would rather keep hidden. Ted Olsen, reporter for *Christianity Today*, has covered a lot of church scandals in his twenty years of journalism, and he is more aware than most of the possibility of false or misleading accusations. Though he is concerned about trials by social media and self-righteous watchdogs, he writes,

Even still (and I hate to use a line from airport-security theater): If you see something, say something. . . . This is not a call for . . . witch-hunting. It's a call for self-examination—and a plea. If you know something, tell someone. If you're hoping that something will resolve itself, you need more fear that it will blow up terribly. If you are praying that God will bring something to light, listen to his call to "take no part in the unfruitful works of darkness, but instead expose them" (Eph. 5:11). When we say something, we help to ensure that dark deeds done in secret can no longer wreak havoc in the lives of the innocent.[13]

13 Ted Olsen, "If You See Something, Say Something," *Christianity Today*, May 8, 2015, https://www.christianitytoday.com/.

This principle applies not only to moral failure among leaders but also to ordinary people carrying out ordinary life activities. We are our brothers' keepers. Russell Moore, former president of the Ethics and Religious Liberty Commission of the Southern Baptist Convention, observes that fake news and conspiracy theories do not merely test our rational abilities but our moral courage as well. He writes: "The problem in this country, and in the church, is not, first, that so many people are falling for crazed and irrational conspiracy theories. The problem is that too many people who do not believe such things are afraid of those people who do."[14] Our biggest problem, according to Moore, is not a failure of credulity but a failure of courage. We suffer from an unwillingness to speak the truth when it might make us feel uncomfortable or lose standing with our friends or in-group. This is primarily a followership failure, not a leadership failure.

More generally, the failure to speak the truth is subtly pervasive in our Christian institutions. It manifests itself within small group Bible studies when no one speaks up after someone advocates for a position that is contrary to Scripture, based on false reports, or unfairly presents the other side. We do not need to verbally flog each other, but we do need to speak up. We are the immune system of the body of Christ for one another—testing every teaching, speaking the truth in love, admonishing the unruly, confronting false teachings and immoral conduct. When we refuse to speak up, the lies grow, the infection spreads, and the body of Christ is corrupted and compromised just like a physical body with an unsound immune system. So, if you see something, say something.

---

14  Russell Moore, "The Gospel in a Democracy Under Assault," *The Gospel Coalition*, January 6, 2021, https://www.thegospelcoalition.org/.

*Bylaws Are Not "Bye, Laws"*

Earlier in this chapter we quoted Andy Crouch's lament over the failure of many churches and organizations to implement basic accountability structures and how this creates a climate in which hidden sins and falsehoods can linger and multiply. Oftentimes, these structures are nominally present within our organizations in the form of bylaws or written procedures—we simply fail to implement them. We act like these rules are suggestions or that they are irrelevant because our organization has good leaders and is doing just fine. In effect, we dismiss them by saying "bye, laws!" to our bylaws.

I (Rick) was meeting with some board members of a school that was having a hard time with a long-standing member who exercised undue influence. I knew the organization had established a structure whereby board members served three-year terms that could be renewed once and, after that, had to cycle off the board for at least one year. This structure allowed entrenched members to be removed with minimal organizational conflict. When I asked when this board member would be cycling off the board, they looked perplexed. When I mentioned this bylaw, they said, "Oh, we haven't done that for years!" The board was simply neglecting the bylaws in their election and nominating procedures because for many years things were going just fine and the organization was thriving. Now, however, the neglected bylaws had come back to haunt them.

In this particular case, the problems that resulted were difficult and irritating, but they were not the sorts of problems that cascade into public scandals or devastate a ministry. However, not everyone is so lucky. Recent sexual scandals that came to light at

Ravi Zacharias International Ministries (RZIM) festered (in part) because of a failure to exercise ordinary due diligence and board oversight. Early accusations came to light but were dismissed. Ruth Malhotra, the public relations manager for RZIM, was concerned that accusations made against Ravi Zacharias by Lori Anne Thompson were not taken seriously. She recounts a conversation with a board member about these accusations, summarizing,

> Board member Bill Payne stated that he and the Board "did not ask Ravi any questions" [with regard to his RICO lawsuit against the Thompsons]. "Why would we, it's Ravi?" Payne explained. When I brought up the fact that Ravi was repeatedly stating to the Task Force that, "The Board has seen everything; I've given them complete access," Payne responded, "Ravi offered us access, but we didn't avail of that access—we didn't feel the need to, it's Ravi."[15]

Again, one can see the pattern of neglecting procedural norms because the ministry is flourishing and the leader is successful, charismatic, and respected. Of course, as time went by and more information came out, explanations grew increasingly implausible. Finally, a full-blown scandal emerged and, as a result, the ministry has been completely devastated. In a case like this, it is hard to project what would have happened if ordinary due diligence had been practiced; we will never know. Due diligence was neglected because of underlying trust in the leader. But bylaws and

---

15 Julie Roys, "Spokesperson's Letter Reveals RZIM's Spiritually Abusive Leadership and Consequences of Protecting 'Ravi' and 'Brand,'" *The Roys Report*, February 15, 2021, https://julieroys.com/.

procedures are written so that they can become habituated into the ordinary practices of institutional life by applying them to all leaders and all members of the organization. They are meant to be part of the daily life of faithful followership. They are not meant to be archived and dusted off for moments when someone seems or is deemed less than trustworthy.

Mars Hill Church, a megachurch in Seattle that has since disbanded, is a perfect example of the importance of bylaws. A multiepisode podcast detailing the rise and fall of the church was recently published by *Christianity Today*. The program ran several hours, but it dedicated an entire hour-long episode to a battle over the creation and implementation of the bylaws for the church.[16] The fallout of these events included the firing and departure of several staff, an investigation and trial of the two elders who raised questions about the bylaws, the restructuring of the elders board, and ultimately the resignation of Senior Pastor Mark Driscoll and collapse of the church itself. It is an unpleasant tale, but it illustrates the tension that exists between charismatic leaders, powerful ministries, and mundane things like bylaws. The bylaws seemed to some like an impediment to effective ministry. Thus the issue at Mars Hill was not just one of a charismatic leader wanting to assert himself but also of a church living in a state of emergency regarding the work of the gospel. They felt that they could not afford to get distracted by procedural minutiae when there were souls to be won. But this sort of thinking leads to only dusting off the bylaws when something goes wrong. Mike Cosper, the lead reporter for the podcast,

16  Mike Cosper, "State of Emergency," *Christianity Today*, August 9, 2021, https://www .christianitytoday.com/.

summarizes the problem well: "The urgency of the mission can make it tempting to change or suspend the rules, but doing so always paves the way for abuse of leadership."[17]

A similar principle applies to annual reviews for senior leadership (and annual reviews in general). They are never convenient, and when things are going well, they are easy to ignore. But such negligence begins to create a culture of unaccountability that can easily become pervasive. Likewise, whistle-blowing structures are also in place in most organizations, but they are often hidden in manuals and never talked about. When a crisis comes, it takes an awful lot of effort to dig up the procedures and go through the proper channels to file the report. The end result is that we habituate our employees or church members to have little or no conscious awareness of the accountability structures that they are obliged to maintain and implement. We are training our people to be poor followers.

## Own Your Mission

Most churches or Christian organizations have a mission statement. If you want to serve your organization by becoming a more faithful follower, you might begin by memorizing its mission statement. Most of us would recognize the mission statement of our organization in a multiple choice test but few of us would do as well if we had to fill in the blank. Take a minute and try it right now. It's not easy, is it?

There is a substantial benefit to internalizing the wording of a mission statement rather than just knowing the general idea.

17 Mike Cosper, "State of Emergency."

For example, we (Joanne and I) both work at Biola University, and our mission is "biblically-centered education, scholarship and service—equipping men and women in mind and character to impact the world for the Lord Jesus Christ."[18] Imagine a faculty member who has not learned the wording of the mission statement but simply knows the general idea that Biola provides Christian education and that they are supposed to integrate faith and learning. If that faculty member were then to evaluate syllabi or lectures by simply asking if they were Christian, a lot of things might pass the test that would never pass the test of being biblically centered. The wording matters.

Internalizing the mission statement helps avoid an overdependence on higher levels of leadership to assure mission fidelity. We are prone to think that the leader tells the followers where they should be headed. This is almost exactly wrong. Followers may lack the knowledge to get to a desired destination but they should know the destination. I was reminded of this recently when talking to a friend who was consulting with a church in crisis. They were trying to hire a new senior pastor but the process had failed and the church was divided. As my friend interviewed various church members, he discovered that most of the congregation were hoping to hire a new pastor quickly so that they could get a new vision for the church. My friend told them that they had gotten the cart before the horse. A congregation cannot find a suitable candidate until they know what they want the candidate to do. One cannot assess ministry fit if one doesn't know what the ministry is. A new pastor and a congregation should come

---

18 "Mission, Vision and Values," Biola University, accessed December 14, 2021, https://www.biola.edu/.

together because they both see and passionately desire the same goals. And of course the same is true when hiring faculty at a university or staff in a Christian ministry.

Ira Chaleff has been writing about the importance of followership for over two decades. He is convinced that the heartbeat of a healthy organization is leaders and followers who exhibit a deep and common ownership of a shared purpose. To illustrate his point, he talks about teachers and students, writing,

> You can't, by definition, have a world of only leaders! To think of leaders without followers is like thinking of teachers without students. . . . They are two sides of one process, two parts of a whole. Teachers and students form a learning circle around a body of knowledge or skills; leaders and followers form an action circle around a common purpose.[19]

Once we realize the mission of the organization must be fully owned by both leaders and followers, it is much easier to see that accountability for accomplishing the mission is a two-way street—followers hold the leader accountable to the mission every bit as much as leaders hold the followers accountable.

If members of a congregation need a clear sense of the mission of the church in order to be faithful followers, surely the same could be said of citizens within a nation. If we are to be faithful voters and participants in our political society, we need to have a clear vision of God's design for politics. We need a well-formed public theology. Otherwise, we will never be able to distinguish

19  Ira Chaleff, *The Courageous Follower: Standing up to and for Our Leaders* (Oakland, CA: Berrett-Koehler Publishers, 2009), 18, ProQuest.

good political leadership from bad. Ed Stetzer, reflecting on the storming of the Capitol Building, noted that Christian participation in these events indicated a lack of political discipleship within the church. We have not taught believers to think theologically about politics. In his words,

All of us have failed to foster healthy political discipleship. . . . Committed to reaching the world, the evangelical movement has emphasized the evangelistic and pietistic elements of the mission. However, it has failed to connect this mission to justice and politics. The result of this discipleship failure has led us to a place where not only our people, but many of our leaders, were easily fooled and co-opted by a movement that ended with the storming of the US Capitol.[20]

Evangelical churches have been good at promoting activism. We are quick to march but slow to think theologically. We have not trained our congregations to have a thoughtful and biblically anchored public theology. In the absence of such anchoring, we are easily blown to and fro by the political storms of our day or by the whims of celebrity leaders. Only well-anchored followers will be able to hold fast to the biblical mission and hold leaders or elected officials accountable to it.

Two additional benefits of owning the mission statement should also be mentioned. First, owning the mission makes creative implementation of the mission much more likely. A person who has internalized the mission statement will find it coming to

20  Stetzer, "Evangelicals Face a Reckoning."

mind when facing a problem or confronted by a new opportunity. It is far more likely that their natural response will be mission-faithful if the mission has become second nature to them. Also, internalizing the mission helps prevent mission drift. I (Rick) recently bought a car that included, among other safety features, an automatic lane departure warning. It gives a slight corrective tug to the wheel when the car begins to drift out of its lane. It is extremely helpful—and I've been shocked to discover how often I feel a little tug on my steering wheel. It seems I've probably been drifting out of my lane much more often than I thought! The same applies to organizations. It is easy to drift away from the mission, so it is wonderful to have an internalized mission statement that gives a little tug on your heart when your daily activities begin to drift out of their missional lane.

## Face Hard Truths

Bestselling business author Jim Collins describes what he calls the Stockdale Paradox as follows: "you must maintain unwavering faith that you can and will prevail in the end, regardless of the difficulties, and at the same time, have the discipline to confront the most brutal facts of your current reality, whatever they might be."[21] He offers Winston Churchill as an example of a person who embraced this paradox. He had an iron will and resolve to fight the Nazis until the earth was rid of their shadow. However, he was equally committed to hard truths, as seen in his creation of the Statistical Office, whose primary mission was to feed him a continuous and unfiltered stream of facts—a brutal but accurate picture of reality.

21  Jim Collins, "Level 5 Leadership: The Triumph of Humility and Fierce Resolve," *Harvard Business Review*, July 1, 2005, https://hbr.org/.

Accomplishing the mission was a cheering and sustaining thought for Churchill but completing the mission lay on the other side of current realities—realities that were often very unpleasant to face.

The Stockdale Paradox makes it clear that we cannot simply be committed to our mission but must also commit to facing the truth. We need the Christian equivalent of the Statistical Office that is committed to telling the unvarnished truth about ourselves and our circumstances. Old Testament prophets served this function for the Old Testament kings—they were completely committed to Israel's mission as God's covenant people but they never faltered when it came to declaring difficult truths. These truths were often unwelcome, yet the prophets had the courage to declare them nonetheless, even if that meant being hunted in the wilderness or thrown into the miry clay at the bottom of a well.

We mentioned earlier that it is easy for organizations to neglect bylaws or fail to follow basic procedures. One of the most common reasons for this is an underlying unwillingness to face inconvenient truths. Whether truths are about moral failures of leadership, poor performance of employees, or ineffectiveness at reaching ministry goals, they must be faced. Ted Olsen, in the article cited earlier, discusses the challenge of speaking up when we see something wrong. He notes that doing so almost always means speaking an unwelcome truth that is likely to be met with resistance. As he puts it, "my experience tells me that organizational leaders dramatically underestimate their capacity to self-deceive and turn a blind eye."[22]

What makes the difficult job of facing the truth even more difficult is that we live in a world that tacitly trains us to reject

---

22  Olsen, "If You See Something, Say Something."

difficult truths. It used to be that media sources were intentionally doing something called "broadcasting"—they were trying to speak to the vast majority of Americans at the same time with the same content. In a broadcast world, we are constantly exposed to views that we do not share. However, recent changes in social media have dramatically altered the way we consume news. Our news sources are now filtered through algorithms designed to continually give us more and more of what we want to hear. The consequences of this are devastating for truth seekers. Our media sources have been customized to tickle our ears. Political analyst Chris Stirewalt made a career of calling elections based on a twofold goal of getting it right and getting it first. He was working for Fox News in the 2020 election and called the state of Arizona for Biden. He turned out to be both right and first, but he ended up being fired for it. Commenting on what he calls the "informational malnourishment" that characterizes our media consumption, he said that

> the competitive advantage belongs to those who can best habituate consumers . . . avoiding at almost any cost impinging on the reality so painstakingly built around them. As outlets have increasingly prioritized habituation over information, consumers have unsurprisingly become ever more sensitive to any interruption of their daily diet. . . . Having been cosseted by self-validating coverage for so long, many Americans now consider any news that might suggest that they are in error or that their side has been defeated *as an attack on them personally.*[23]

23 Chris Stirewalt, "I Called Arizona for Biden on Fox News. Here's What I Learned," *Los Angeles Times*, January 28, 2021, https://www.latimes.com/; emphasis added.

In other words, we have conditioned ourselves to eat the journalistic equivalent of junk food. We live on a constant diet of stories selected for us because they will taste good, not because they are true or important. As a result we have become conditioned to resent and reject unwelcome truth. We have cultivated a malnourished mind.

## Value Faithfulness over Success

More subtle than the temptation to reject difficult truths is our desire to seek favor and success. To an extent, it is simply natural to want to please people and be well regarded by others. It seems to be hardwired into human beings. But the danger is that our desire for success trumps our calling to be faithful followers. Paul puts the matter clearly when confronting the Galatians: "If I were still trying to please man, I would not be a servant of Christ" (Gal. 1:10).

No Christian would say that they care more about worldly success than the favor of God, but it is amazingly easy to fall into this trap. Sometimes it is simply because we are tired of feeling neglected, disregarded, or disdained by the watching world. We crave just a bit of recognition or acknowledgment. Especially when evangelicalism is at odds with the cultural elites, it is a satisfying feeling to taste their favor. Chuck Colson, reflecting on his pre-Watergate days in the White House, noticed this phenomenon:

> When I served under President Nixon, one of my jobs was to work with special-interest groups, including religious leaders. We would invite them to the White House, wine and dine them, take them on cruises aboard the presidential yacht . . .

Ironically, few were more easily impressed than religious leaders. The very people who should have been immune to the worldly pomp seemed most vulnerable.[24]

Influence, power, financial gain, and celebrity are seductive— not just to bad people but also to good ones. It is not just that we are tempted by worldly gain or that we cross God-given boundaries. A faithful servant of God wants to be a part of a successful ministry. We want to have a ten-talent return on what God has given us. When a ministry is thriving, it is extremely difficult to speak up when we see something wrong. If you work in a successful church or Christian ministry then your paycheck is at stake, but even if you are just a member of the congregation or a volunteer in a ministry, there is a lot to lose. David French, Christian attorney and journalist, notes that those who are a part of successful organizations are "admired in part because the founder is admired. They have influence in part because the founder has influence. When the founder fails, they lose more than a paycheck. There is powerful personal incentive to circle the wagons and to defend the ministry, even when that defense destroys lives."[25]

The tendency to draw status from our leaders is nothing new. Michelle Lee-Barnewall sees this same pattern in 1 Corinthians. It seems the Corinthians were seeking human prestige by seeking attachment to a successful spiritual leader. Their leader's status added to their status. But Paul strongly rejects this desire. Lee-Barnewall explains that

24  Quoted in Stetzer, "Evangelicals Face a Reckoning."
25  David French, "'You Are One Step Away from Complete and Total Insanity,'" *The Dispatch*, February 14, 2021, https://frenchpress.thedispatch.com/.

in contrast to the Corinthians' emphasis on the status of the apostles . . . Paul reverses the situation by lowering the apostles' status . . . [they] are a "spectacle to the world," "the scum of the world," and the "dregs of all things" (1 Cor. 4:9–13). Rather than enjoying the privileges of a superior position, they are "without honor," "hungry and thirsty," "poorly clothed," "roughly treated," "homeless," "reviled," and "persecuted" (1 Cor. 4:10–12). Like Christ, they are "fools" and "weak" in the eyes of the world (v. 10), but according to God they are workers who help to build and care for his holy temple (1 Cor. 3:9–17). Paul is not simply saying that they are leaders who have the attitude of a servant. He asserts that as servants they are the opposite of what the world esteems in status, privilege, and other worldly considerations.[26]

Christian leaders and Christian followers alike need to become disenchanted with worldly success—not just in the sense of money and power but also in the sense of the prestige and status that are received for being part of a successful ministry in our present world. And then we need to become re-enchanted with ordinary faithfulness and the prospect of hearing the praise of Jesus himself—"Well done, thou good and faithful servant!" (Matt. 25:21 KJV).

## Exercise Your Conscience

One of the greatest gifts that followers can offer a ministry is a well-formed conscience. We don't speak nearly enough about

26 Michelle Lee-Barnewall, *Neither Complementarian Nor Egalitarian: A Kingdom Corrective to the Evangelical Gender Debate* (Grand Rapids, MI: Baker Academic, 2016), 109.

conscience these days, and it would be good to give a quick re-fresher. A conscience tastes actions, real or potential, and renders a judgment of good or bad in much the same way our tongues judge food to be sweet or sour. The conscience is an internal moral sense. It is a gift of God, and having a moral conscience is part of what it means to bear God's image. The divine origin of our conscience also leads to a second function of our conscience—it serves as an indicator of our self-perceived standing before God. In this sense, our conscience tastes not merely an action or set of actions but the whole of our person. It gives us sense of how we, as persons, stand before God: guilty or not guilty. Thus, the term "conscience" provides a way to speak about the integrity of a person; to act against conscience is perceived as wrong because it violates a person's integrity.

The deeply personal and individual nature of conscience pro-vides a profoundly important check and balance to the corporate culture and policies of any organization. Organizations are made up of people who come together to accomplish a shared purpose, but unity of purpose does not assure unanimity of conscience. And it should be noted that this is a good thing not a bad thing. Policies are often set in abstract or in response to particular needs, but the outworking of those policies is found in particu-lar actions done by particular people. These actions often take place in unanticipated contexts and they often have unforeseen consequences. Therefore, a vital function of each person within an organization is to exercise their conscience as they carry out particular assignments or enforce policy directives. Individuals need their conscience to taste these actions and see if they are good or bad. Policies are established in conference rooms but lived out on the frontlines, so feedback about unanticipated contexts and unforeseen consequences is absolutely vital. And, of course, it is followers who populate the frontlines, so they must become the conduits of feedback.

A conscience is given by God, but it is developed by its owner. We can cultivate it or sear it; we can listen to it or suppress it. For Christians, it is particularly important that our thinking not be conformed to the world but rather transformed by the renewing of our minds, for it is only in this way that we can discern the will of God, according to Romans 12:2. It is passages like this that led Martin Luther to famously declare at his heresy trial in 1521, "I am bound by the Scriptures I have quoted and my conscience is captive to the Word of God."[27] Faithful followers seek to bind their consciences to the word of God.

Unfortunately binding one's conscience to the word of God is not always as easy as it sounds because God says some difficult things. For example, Paul and Peter clearly state that we ought not return evil for evil (Rom. 12:17) or revile others when they revile us (1 Pet. 2:23). But these commands and the corresponding example of Jesus himself often seem painfully remote when we are in the midst of an ugly conflict. Daniel Taylor, Christian scholar and author, states this problem well. He notes that we live in a hostile world and a lot of that hostility is directed toward Christians. Unfortunately, we too often yield to the temptation to return that hostility in kind: "The sad truth is that, in our battle with a hostile culture, we have adopted the culture's tactics. We fight ugliness with ugliness, distortion with distortion, sarcasm

---

27 Martin Luther, *Faith and Freedom: An Invitation to the Writings of Martin Luther* (New York: Vintage, 2002), 20.

with sarcasm."[28] He goes on to observe that this is not just a tactical failure—it is a failure of discipleship. It is an unwillingness to make pleasing God our first thing. He explains,

> I believe we [adopt the culture's tactics] because we do not really trust the gospel. *Turn the other cheek, the first shall be last, lose our life to gain it, love our enemies.* Those bold principles of Jesus make for great sermons, but in our bones, we appear not to believe they are practical for everyday living in a hostile society. We seem to believe that if we are not as aggressive and hard-nosed as our supposed enemies, that God (and our organization) will somehow be defeated and goodness will disappear from the earth.[29]

Taylor is suggesting that we don't really believe that pleasing God works. It doesn't pay—or perhaps it only pays when other people are being nice too. And when we feel like it doesn't pay, we fear that we have to reshape ourselves into our culture's image in order to succeed. But when we do this, we are effectively saying that temporal success is more important to us than fidelity to the gospel. One might call this the unbinding of one's conscience from the word of God. And Taylor's example is particularly helpful because it points out that conscience does not only apply to a particular course of action or an intended goal but also the means by which that goal is achieved. It is the work of conscience to remind us that we dare not violate God's word on the way to achieving a good goal.

28  Daniel Taylor, "Are You Tolerant? (Should You Be?)," *Christianity Today*, January 17, 1999, https://www.christianitytoday.com/.
29  Taylor, "Are You Tolerant?"

## Conclusion

In summary, leadership and followership must share responsibility for the crisis of our day, and our crisis will only be resolved by increasing the dedication and devotion of both leaders and followers. More specifically, our long neglect of followership and lack of a vision for excellence in following must end. We must intentionally develop followers who own their mission, face hard truths, value faithfulness over success, exercise their conscience, and are willing to speak up when they see things go wrong. This is not easy but, fortunately, we can find instructive examples from some of the followers who have walked this path before us.

# Glimpses of Faithful Following

*The fellowship of being near unto God must become
reality, . . . it must permeate and give color to our feeling,
our perceptions, our sensations, our thinking , our
imagining, our willing, our acting, our speaking. It must
not stand as a foreign factor in our life, but it must be
the passion that breathes throughout our whole existence.*

SØREN KIERKEGAARD, *PROVOCATIONS*

LIVING IN A WORLD THAT RARELY IDENTIFIES or rewards following makes it much harder to conceive of what good following really looks like. Of course, we have already looked at biblical examples like Jesus and Paul and discovered that they are actually every bit as good as examples of followership as they are of leadership. But Jesus and Paul are extraordinary people by any measure, and they also lived in a very different time and place. It is helpful to have a few glimpses of average people who are closer to us in time and place.

## Abraham Kuyper and His Congregation

We will begin our glimpses of good followers with the story of the members of the first church served by the famed Dutch theologian Abraham Kuyper. Kuyper ultimately became one of the most influential Christians of late nineteenth-century Europe. He founded a newspaper, a university, and a religious denomination. He also founded a political party and was even elected prime minister of the Netherlands. His guiding light was an all-consuming passion for living out his Calvinist convictions in every sphere of life that he touched. Thus, it is shocking to discover that this great leader's most important influence came from the faithful and committed followers at his first church posting.

Kuyper had completed a stellar academic career by earning a PhD in theology from the University of Leyden. But during this time, he also shed the pious faith of his upbringing in favor of the modern liberal theology he was taught at university. Upon graduation, he was ordained and sent to the small northern fishing village of Beesd. Things did not go well. The congregation was anchored to the very doctrines and mission he had abandoned. Not surprisingly, he attempted to educate these backward-thinking folks and enlighten them to the truths of the modern world. But God and his people had other plans. Kuyper began meeting with some of the discontented individuals and was amazed at how deeply rooted they were in the Scriptures and how they were even more knowledgeable about traditional theology than he was. In fact, to return to the language of the previous chapter, it would be hard to find a set of people who more firmly owned their own mission. They were committed to the gospel and saw the liberal theology that Kuyper was presenting to be a clear departure from it. As Kuyper spoke more and more with this group of church members, he found something awakening within his own heart. He had to decide if he would resist or join them. Years later he reflected on this critical moment and said, "I did not oppose them and I still thank God that I made that choice. Their unremitting perseverance has become the blessing of my heart, the rise of the morning star in my life."[1]

One of Kuyper's biographers, George Puchinger, views this moment as Kuyper's second conversion, saying, "no one can understand the Kuyper he became without realizing that his decisive confessional transformation was not an academic conversion, but a religious one, which happened through the talks with the simplest farmers and laborers of Beesd, who pointed him the way spiritually."[2] This was a group of followers, but they were followers who knew their mission and calling. They had a clear direction. If their pastor seemed to be headed in a different direction, they needed to make him aware of that problem. Simply put, if not for a small congregation of devout followers, Kuyper's gifts and tremendous energy might have been spent on activities far removed from advancing God's kingdom.

## Le Chambon

Another glimpse of followership comes from a tiny French town by the name of Le Chambon. During the Nazi occupation of France, this village of about three thousand people was responsible for saving as many as six thousand Jewish refugees by offering

1  Abraham Kuyper, *Lectures on Calvinism* (Grand Rapids, MI: Eerdmans, 1961), vi.
2  George Puchinger, *Abraham Kuyper: His Early Journey of Faith*, ed. George Harnick, trans. Simone Kennedy (Amsterdam: VU University, 1998), 26–27.

them a safe haven in their own homes and then passage to Switzerland. It was an extremely dangerous task, one that all too few people were willing to take up—even devout Christians.

Phillip Hallie writes about this village in his moving book *Lest Innocent Blood Be Shed*. He travelled to the village while writing it and found a place of cheerful simplicity. But the villagers had more to them than met the eye. They had a deep attachment to their ancient Huguenot heritage. Centuries of persecution had blessed these Huguenots with a mentality of perseverance, even in extremely difficult times, and also provided countless good examples of sacrificial commitment to a cause. They were also providentially blessed with a powerful leader, André Trocmé, who ended up playing a very significant role in the events that unfolded. His service cannot be overstated. But without the ordinary villagers, there would be no story to tell.

Hallie interviewed these villagers at length. The stories they told were deeply moving. But what was most striking to Hallie was their almost complete inability to see themselves as moral heroes or even as particularly good. As he described it, they were prone to say things like, "Why are you calling us good? We were doing what had to be done. Who else could help them? And what has all this to do with goodness? Things had to be done, that's all, and we happened to be there to do them. You must understand it was the most natural thing in the world to help these people."[3]

The citizens of Le Chambon did not traffic in elaborate explanations. Nor were they people who had taken up what they viewed to be some vast and noble moral enterprise. They were not

---

3   Philip Paul Hallie, *Lest Innocent Blood Be Shed: The Story of the Village of Le Chambon and How Goodness Happened There* (New York: HarperPerennial, 1994), 20–21.

eloquent when it came to explaining why they did what they did. And generally, their strategies for how they did what they did were spontaneous and simple. They just took people into their homes, schools, hotels, and outbuildings. They brought them food and then they provided what they needed to get to a safe place. They knew that helpless people needed help. They knew that hunted people needed protection. They knew that a person at your door was a person that you could not turn away. To them, it was all common sense, as well as a demand incumbent upon people who follow Jesus. They were simply obliged to care for "the least of these" (Matt. 25:40).

Perhaps, at that time and place, the most remarkable thing they understood was that a Jewish person was still a person. Even more importantly, they expressed this truth in practical action. Often, these actions could not have been planned ahead of time or commanded by a leader. The situation demanded followers who owned and understood the mission that Jews had to be helped and sheltered from those who were pursuing and persecuting them. Hallie explains,

> There were seven boarding houses, over a dozen pensions, and even more scattered peasant farms which sheltered refugees. No Chambonnais turned away a refugee or betrayed one. There was one successful police raid which caught a number of refugee children, but usually the police found nothing. "Jews? What would Jews be doing here? You, there, have you seen any Jews? They say they have a hooked nose."[4]

4   Hallie, *Lest Innocent Blood Be Shed*, 161.

Similarly, their leader Pastor Trocmé said, "We do not know what a Jew is, we know only human beings."[5] People were helped purely and simply because they were human beings in need. Trocmé's wife Magda put it this way:

> Those of us who received the first Jews did what we thought had to be done—nothing more complicated. . . . There were many people in the village who needed help. How could we refuse them? . . . We had no time to think. When a problem came, we had to solve it immediately. . . . There was no decision to make. The issue was: Do you think we are all brothers or not? Do you think it is unjust to turn in the Jews or not? Then let us try to help![6]

The role of Trocmé's leadership should not be minimized, but there was a strong resolve among these villagers quite independently of Trocmé himself. They were devout Christians, even if they lacked sophistication. They loved their pastor just as their pastor loved them. When Trocmé came to the church a few years before World War II began, he was clear about his pacifist convictions. This was fine with the congregation, even though not all of them shared his pacifism. But when France mobilized for war, Pastor Trocmé felt obliged to step down. Pacifism was not common among French Protestants, and he did not want to complicate the life of the church during such turbulent times. The church council, thinking for itself, did not see the need, so they simply refused to accept his resignation. A few short years later, a

5  Hallie, *Lest Innocent Blood Be Shed*, 161.
6  Hallie, *Lest Innocent Blood Be Shed*, 20–21.

national leader of the Reformed Church demanded that Trocmé stop aiding Jews because it could damage French Protestantism. Trocmé refused and again tendered his resignation. Once again, the council refused to accept it. The members of the church were simply committed to loving God and loving their neighbor. Their pastor was leading them to do that, and they had no interest in seeing him dismissed—whatever the political, philosophical, or theological arguments might be.

Ultimately, the story of Le Chambon became one of the few shining moments of Christian faithfulness in the otherwise dark story of the Holocaust. The example of these believers should never be forgotten, both for the sake of the many lives they saved and also for the inspiration they offer us even today of the tremendous importance of faithful followership in extraordinarily difficult times.

### Church of the Saviour

"The story of the Church of the Saviour is a very disturbing story. It makes most of us ashamed of our mild Christianity."[7] So writes Elizabeth O'Connor in her book *Call to Commitment*, which recounts the history of the Church of the Saviour in Washington, DC. As we shall discover shortly, she is certainly right. It is a story that is likely to make a person ashamed of mild Christianity. It is, however, also a story that gives a compelling glimpse of what it looks like for the ordinary members of a church—not the leaders—to take seriously the call of Christ as faithful followers.

---

7   Elizabeth O'Connor, *Call to Commitment: The Story of the Church of the Saviour, Washington, D.C.* (New York: Harper & Row, 1975), xi.

The Church of the Saviour was founded by Gordon and Mary Cosby in 1947 in Washington, DC. Gordon Cosby was just returning from serving in the European theater during WWII, and he had been profoundly impacted by his experience. Cosby had served as a chaplain but he was on the front lines. He was part of the invasion of Normandy on D-Day. He pulled wounded soldiers to safety, ministered to the dying, and buried his best friend on those beaches. He was awarded a Silver Star for bravery. One of the great lessons he took away from his experience was the woefully inadequate preparation given these GIs by the churches they were a part of. O'Connor explains,

> As [Cosby] dealt with young men who were facing death, he realized how poorly equipped they were to deal with the questions of life and death and how poor their faith had prepared them. And it was that experience that convinced him to—if he survived the war—come back to the states and . . . start a church.[8]

The Church of the Saviour became known for many things. It was one of the first places of interracial worship in the city. It founded over forty ministries that served the needs of Washington, DC and the surrounding area. It shaped the ministry of countless other churches—many of which became larger and better known. Several renowned Christian leaders came to regard Cosby as a mentor and guide. But this is the fruit of the ministry, not the root. The root was a profound sense of the significance of Christian followership. Cosby had seen dozens of soldiers who had been committed

8    Lily Percy, "Pastor, Mentor And Social Activist: Remembering Gordon Cosby," *Weekend All Things Considered (NPR)*, April 14, 2013, EBSCO.

church attenders but had a faith that was almost irrelevant to how they lived their lives, so he became determined to build a church that was full of people who understood the transcendent importance of following Jesus. It is well worth taking a look at how he did this.

## High View of the Christian Call to Discipleship

Above all else, Gordon Cosby viewed the Christian life as extremely demanding for everyone, not just for pastors or apostles or heroes of the faith. This had become second nature to him through his various formative life experiences, but he soon realized that this was not a common view. Years after his service in the war, he explained his view on following in response to a question asked him by a student at Baylor University:

Q: Gordon, you make it sound so easy, but I know it's not. I can talk about following, but am I ever going to be willing to do so? As the church, are we willing to make the commitment to follow in this kind of way? I guess that's the real challenge of the Gospel.

A: That's right. What Jesus said, and what we say to each other is, "Are we talking about something important or is it just talk?" That is what Jesus was doing with the people who said, "I want to follow you." He would ask the people who said they wanted to follow if they really did. They were deciding if they would get in the boat with Jesus. He was so clear in saying, "Let's think about it first."[9]

9   Gordon Cosby and Jon E. Singletary, "An Interview with Gordon Cosby: Co-Founder of the Church of the Saviour," *Family and Community Ministries* 21, no. 2 (January 1, 2007): 35.

For Cosby, the most important question every person has to answer is about following: Is following Christ something important or is it "just talk"? For him the answer was clear, and he felt that it should be clear for every Christian. Following Christ is our first and most important call.

## High View of Church Membership

Therefore, when it came to organizing the Church of the Saviour, membership commitments were high. Cosby expresses this vision eloquently when he says,

> We understand the Christian Church as the gathering of those who are committed to Christ and to one another in the living of a common life. We are to be pioneers, missionaries, evangelists, teachers, and prophets-representatives of the new humanity. The proclamation of the gospel is not alone for a little official group of people which is called clergy. It is for all who have met the Pioneer and Perfecter of our faith, who know that Christ is on the march.[10]

This view of what it means to be a member of a church was a major change from what many other churches practiced. It was nothing like the low bar of mere verbal profession that is common in many denominations. But of course, that was exactly the point. The church that Cosby was planting was in response to the gross inadequacies he had seen in the faith of the many soldiers he had known in the war. Cosby and the other founders of Church of the

---

10  O'Connor, *Call to Commitment*, 23.

Saviour felt that "the profound meanings of membership need to be rethought. Surely entrance into the Christian Church presupposes total commitment to Christ as the Lord of the church."[11]

Their perspective on the significance of following Christ was also reflected in their approach to evangelism. It had to be. They felt that if the church was to have integrity of membership, they must have a similar integrity in evangelism. O'Connor summarizes their approach as follows:

> The student is presented, in present-day terminology, the laws of the spirit as taught by Jesus. He is urged to disprove them if he can, but in any case, to try them. The point is especially emphasized that, rather than blindly accepting the claim that Jesus is the Son of the Living God or flatly denying it, the student is to try living with Him for six months. . . . we [must] present the unmistakable implications of deep and total commitment involved in following Christ—the challenge and risk and danger, the promise and the cost.[12]

With an approach like this, both evangelism and church membership had substance and integrity. Membership was a costly decision—it involved attending the School of Christian Living, which included classes on Old and New Testament, Christian growth, ethics, and doctrine, taught in regular rotation. It also required entering into a mentor relationship with a person who was already a member. Those who joined were also making a commitment to regular giving (starting with a tithe) and serving

11  O'Connor, *Call to Commitment*, 25.
12  O'Connor, *Call to Commitment*, 26.

within one of the ministry groups in the church. It was a process that took at least two years of preparation because it was felt that it took time for a person to truly be ready to make a commitment "to give [Christ] a practical priority in all the affairs of life."[13] This membership commitment was renewed every year at a church-wide service.

## High View of the Spirit's Ability to Deploy Ordinary People for Ministry

One additional aspect of the Church of the Saviour deserves attention. Since the commitment to membership entailed a commitment to serving in a mission group, there had to be a lot of mission groups. Indeed, the church has had more than 40 of these groups over the years though it never had a membership of more than about 120 persons. How did all these groups arise? Cosby was fiercely committed to the notion that the essence of Christian ministry is the ministry of the layperson. In a 1957 brochure describing the School of Christian Living, Cosby wrote,

It is often said that the Church must leave the churches and go into the market place and workshop, there to hear witness to the power of Christ to bring meaning into life. "But the fact is," says the Evanston Report of the World Council of Churches, "the church is already in these places. How? In the persons of its laymen." It is the laymen who are fighting the real battles of faith in factories, shops, offices and farms, in political parties and government agencies, in countless homes, in the press,

13  Marjory Zoet-Bankson, "A History of the Church of the Saviour," *Eighth Day Faith Community*, accessed September 23, 2021, https://8th-day.org/.

radio and television, and in the relationships of nations. If the laymen do not bear witness to the faith in these places, then there will be no witness.[14]

At Church of the Saviour, mission groups are driven by the followership, not the leadership. There is no waiting for top-down initiative; rather, individual members sense the leading of the Spirit to meet particular needs. O'Connor describes this process as she offers her explanation of what mission groups really are:

> What is meant by a mission group? The Church is a people which is sharing in the mission of Jesus Christ. . . . As I discover what aspect of that mission is mine, and as you discover your mission, and they happen to coincide, then we become part of a mission group. It is that simple . . . Who cares what form it takes? Who knows what the details of it will be, when it meets and how it goes about its task? This is not important. The important thing is that this group discover the guidance of God step by step, and be so attuned to His will, and so flexible that it shall be able to discover what He has in mind.[15]

Notice the profound dependence on individual members' abilities to perceive the guidance of the Holy Spirit in the initiation of their ministries. This same posture is adopted when considering the leadership of the ministry as a whole. Because Cosby was a strong leader, and because he cast a distinctive vision from the very first days of Church of the Saviour, it is natural to ask what

14  Zoet-Bankson, "A History of the Church of the Saviour."
15  O'Connor, *Call to Commitment*, 49.

would happen if he was no longer there. O'Connor considered this question back in the early years of the church, and her answer is rather striking:

> What would happen to the Church of the Saviour if it lost not its building but its minister? It is asked by those persons who feel that the Church of the Saviour exists as [a] vital fellowship because Gordon Cosby has brought to it unusual gifts of leadership. Our answer is, "We don't know." We have asked ourselves this lonely question and have decided that we would just gather together and pray, and wait for the Holy Spirit to guide us.[16]

Clearly, she is not offering a succession plan; she is simply describing the way the church members have habituated themselves to ask and answer the important questions they face on a daily basis. They are all followers, and they need to have guidance. So they come together, they pray, and they wait for the Holy Spirit to give the guidance that they need.

Before leaving our consideration of these three churches, it is worthwhile to ask what all these followers have in common. Certainly they find themselves in very different circumstances. Some are living in the midst of a war; others are enjoying peace. Some live in remote rural areas; others live in bustling urban metropolises. Some are called to address biblical and theological fidelity, while others work for justice and oppose oppression. Some of these narratives are spontaneous responses to urgent

---

16 O'Connor, *Call to Commitment*, 41.

circumstances, and others tell the story of the deliberate pursuit of a course of action. Nonetheless, some striking similarities emerge from these diverse narratives:

1. All three of these stories are about relatively unknown churches and anonymous church members. None are really household names except perhaps Abraham Kuyper, and the story we told happened long before he became famous. Church of the Saviour is fairly well-known in certain circles, but it is hardly a Willow Creek or Saddleback. The point is that faithful followers do remarkable things but they often fly under the radar. If you want to have celebrity in our culture, you'll need charismatic leadership, impressive size, lots of money, and influence to boot. If you want to be a faithful follower, just be a faithful follower and let the celebrity chips fall where they may.

2. All three of these churches had strong leadership and strong followers. Their leaders may not have had celebrity status but they were strong and competent. At the same time, all three churches had remarkably strong followers. These ordinary church members played essential parts in accomplishing an extraordinary mission. They did not do this as a stepping-stone to becoming a leader—presumably all the followers we have talked about remained in non-leadership status even after these events. Followership was not a way station or a waiting room for these believers. It is also clear from these stories that strong leadership is fully compatible with strong followership. In fact, it would seem that both blossom more fully in the presence of the other.

3. All these church members elevate our expectations of followership. Followership becomes demanding, meaningful, and inspiring on their watch. For those who can't imagine why followership is worth studying or why one would bother to train people to be good followers, these stories offer a much needed cure.

4. In all of these cases, the initiative, courage, and wisdom of followers is on full display. They enhance the vision and advance the mission of their church. Their energy enabled the church to accomplish things that would be completely impossible with half-hearted followership.

5. These followers are also great examples of the qualities we mentioned in the previous chapter. They internalized and owned their organization's mission at a personal level, faced the hard truths that confronted them, sought the favor of God rather than people, and were willing to speak up even in the face of opposition and persecution.

To round out our glimpses of followership, we will enter the fictional world of C. S. Lewis. One might doubt that fiction could help us face the real-world challenges of followership, but it is actually quite instructive. One of the consistent themes in our book is that our thoughts about following have an extremely low ceiling. In fact, it is not really a matter of a ceiling at all—our thinking it pretty much confined to a mental cellar. And fiction often does a wonderful job of breaking thoughts out of their cellars. When authors create a fictional world, they are not really telling us about a world that doesn't exist but rather the world that exists right under our noses, which we are strangely unable to see. It seems that it sometimes takes a trip to a fantasy world to recognize important features of our real world. This is certainly the case when it comes to our thinking about followership.

The plot of Lewis's fantasy tale *The Silver Chair* revolves around the rescue of Prince Rillian who is held captive by the Queen of the Underworld. The two heroes of the story, Jill and Eustace, are sent by Aslan (the Jesus figure) to free the prince. Aslan appoints a character by the name of Puddleglum as their companion. Puddleglum is a Marsh-wiggle, a very human-like creature except for his frog-like feet and hands, which are well adapted to living in marshes. Puddleglum turns out to be a sturdy companion but not particularly inspiring—he is hard working and faithful but also somewhat gloomy in disposition. For our purposes, we might say he appears to be the perfect example of the low-ceiling follower.

When these companions finally find the prince and attempt to free him, the Queen of the Underworld discovers them and uses smoke from a magic fire to seduce them into wanting to stay in the Underworld. She soothingly dismantles all they have previously believed, assuring them that there is no such thing as the Overworld. The magic smoke numbs their reasoning, and their foggy minds can't seem to come up with any argument to defeat her claims. They are about to yield to the evil Queen when Puddleglum suddenly steps forward, summons his courage, and stamps out the magic fire. At this point, the witch screams in outrage and the others begin to regain their reason. But most important is what happens to Puddleglum. Lewis writes,

The pain made Puddleglum's head for a moment perfectly clear and he knew exactly what he really thought. . . . "One word, Ma'am," he said, coming back from the fire; limping, because of the pain. "One word. All you've been saying is quite right, I shouldn't wonder. . . . But there's one thing more to be said, even so. Suppose we have only dreamed, or made up, all those things—trees and grass and sun and moon and stars and Aslan himself. Suppose we have. Then all I can say is that, in that case, the made-up things seem a good deal more important than the real ones. Suppose this black pit of a kingdom of yours is the only world. Well, it strikes me as a pretty poor one. . . . We're just babies making up a game, if you're right. But four babies playing a game can make a playworld which licks your real world hollow. That's why I'm going to stand by the play-world. I'm on Aslan's side even if there isn't any Aslan to lead it. I'm going to live as like a Narnian as I can even if there isn't any Narnia. So, thanking you kindly for our supper, if these two gentlemen and the young lady are ready, we're leaving your court at once and setting out in the dark to spend our lives looking for Overland. Not that our lives will be very long, I should think; but that's a small loss if the world's as dull a place as you say."[17]

In this, Lewis offers a perfect example of an often invisible but extremely valuable quality of a good follower. Puddleglum cannot win a debate with the evil Queen. At best, he might be able to drum up a reason or two for why the Overworld exists, but he

17  C. S. Lewis, *The Silver Chair* (New York: Scholastic Inc, 1987), 159.

doesn't offer any. In fact, he seems to doubt his reasons would be persuasive. But, as Lewis puts it, "he knew exactly what he really thought." In other words, Puddleglum may not have cut an imposing figure, and he wasn't a charismatic orator. If leadership means vision casting, he was probably in trouble. But what he lacked in eloquence he more than made up for in clarity. He knew things. In fact, he knew quite a lot of things, and he knew them all the way down to the deepest fibers of his soul. He knew that the Queen's world was a hollow, empty, hopeless place where no one could survive. He knew that disobeying the Queen would likely cost them their lives. He knew that the risk was worth it. In short, he knew that they had to flee. Puddleglum didn't know why all these things were true— at least he could not articulate a good reason why. Neither did he know what to do about the trial that confronted him, for the others had to lead the group to safety. But he knew that something had to be done, so he did what little he could do—he stomped out the fire.

One of the great services faithful followers offer organizations, communities, and their families is a clear and simple grasp of the mission. The firmness of their grasp not only offers a positive energy that helps accomplish the mission but also one that resists mission deviation. Puddleglum's sort of following, when it is at its best, is entirely open to innovation but extremely resistant to deviation. The members of Kuyper's church in Beesd are the perfect example of this sort of resistance to deviation. Surely their new pastor could outtalk them, and surely he was the master of all that was new, but they immediately realized that his talk and his newness were a deviation, not an innovation. Also, a faithful follower will often know that certain behaviors simply must not be done, quite independent of the potential impact on the mission or the reputation of a leader. People who are working lower down the leadership structure of an organization often see things going on that are not right. They may not know why these things are going on, and they may not even know the impact these activities are having (for good or for ill), but they do know that these activities should not be going on. It is followers like these who speak up when a key leader is lapsing into moral failure, bullying and abusing others, or financially exploiting his congregation, organization, and key donors. In the spirit of Puddleglum, they simply say that it cannot be allowed, even if they do not have a plan for dealing with the fallout of losing such a leader.

## Conclusion

These stories should help us gain a better picture of what it really looks like when a set of followers take their job seriously. Notice that in all of these cases there was actually good leadership in place. Strong leaders and good followers work very well with each other. Sometimes a good leader like Abraham Kuyper is in need of substantial correction from the followers God puts around them. In other cases, strong and capable leaders like André Trocmé and Gordon Cosby were headed in the right direction but never could have accomplished their mission if not for being surrounded by equally gifted and committed followers. The point, of course, is that both leading and following are absolutely vital to God's work, and the success of God's work depends on all of us doing our part with our whole heart.

# Still I Will Follow

*It is well known that Christ consistently used
the expression "follower." He never asks for
admirers, worshippers, or adherents. No, he
calls disciples. It is not adherents of a teaching
but followers of a life Christ is looking for.*

SØREN KIERKEGAARD, *PROVOCATIONS*

THERE IS SOMETHING STRANGE, almost paradoxical, about our
attitude toward followership. We have discussed the common
stereotypes that trivialize or disparage followers. But there is
another conception of the follower that lurks in our subconscious as well. If we are pressed to come up with a positive
image of following, we are prone to overcorrect. We imagine
the faithful followers of the early church refusing to deny Jesus
even at risk of being fed to lions. We imagine Martin Luther
standing before a tribunal and refusing to recant his teaching.
We imagine Jim Elliot and his colleagues pierced by spears in the

South American rainforest. All these are inspiring stories that make great sermon illustrations, but at times I (Rick) wonder if there is a danger of these images actually distorting our view of faithful following.

The simple fact is that for most of us, though we might be inspired by such sermon illustrations on Sunday morning, our Monday morning does not bring with it the prospect of martyrdom. The cross before us is no worse than going to a job we find dreary, mundane, or demeaning but must go to for the sake of our family. Or perhaps we face the prospect of another day chasing toddlers around our living room or caring for an aging parent who no longer remembers our name or teaching middle school students who have no interest in remembering their lessons. Our hands and feet are not pierced with nails; our lifeblood does not drain from our side. If our life were a movie, it wouldn't be *The Passion of the Christ* or *The Mission*, it would be *Groundhog Day*. We are tested by the relentless assault of daily deeds done to meet our daily needs; our most ominous threat is the likelihood that these needs will rise to face us again tomorrow morning. What does it mean to follow Jesus Christ in such an ordinary life?

## Finding Our Role Models in the Kitchen

Broadening our examples of genuine obedience might help us answer this question. Let me compare and contrast the stories of two of my favorite role models. The first is a classic martyr story. Saint Lawrence was a deacon in the church in Rome during the persecutions of Emperor Valerian in AD 258. One of the first victims of the persecution was Lawrence's beloved mentor,

Pope Sixtus II. After Sixtus II was killed, the Roman authorities arrested Lawrence and then commanded him to hand over the Christians' poor fund. He agreed to do it but asked for three days to accomplish the task. Once freed, Lawrence distributed this much-desired fund among Rome's poor and crippled, many of whom he gathered before the authorities at the close of his three days, proclaiming that "this is the church's treasure, these poor who are rich in their faith."[1] Rome, expecting a cash gift, was disappointed. According to church tradition, the authorities had Lawrence roasted alive on a white-hot gridiron.

It is a powerful story and I stand in awe of believers like Saint Lawrence, but, as I have said, that doesn't change the fact that the only grill I'm likely to face is in my backyard. And yet, perhaps that is the point. Perhaps cooking is exactly where I should be looking for my inspiration. Church history does not cut all its characters from a single cloth. This is where my second role model comes in. Consider the story of Nicholas Herman, a man who was born in eastern France in 1611. He grew up in poverty, so as a young man he served as a soldier to earn his food and shelter. Unfortunately, his leg was wounded in battle and he had to get a job as a footman, opening carriage doors and waiting on tables. At age forty he had a deep spiritual experience and decided to join a monastery—not as a monk but simply as a lay brother assigned to the kitchen. He describes his duties on one particular day as follows: "Recently I went to Burgundy to buy the wine provisions for the society which I have joined. This was a very unwelcome task for me. I have no natural business ability and,

1    Vincent Carroll and David Shiflett, *Christianity On Trial: Arguments Against Anti-Religious Bigotry* (New York: Encounter Books, 2002), 144.

being lame, I cannot get around the boat except by rolling myself over the casks."[2]

It is a sad story. Not only is his job rather boring but he is also ill-suited to it because of his injured leg. Performing his duties is not only dull but also humiliating, requiring him to roll himself over the casks to get where he needed to go. But surprisingly enough, he is undaunted by the experience. Nicholas explains,

> Nonetheless, this matter gave me no uneasiness, nor did the purchase of wine. I told the Lord that it was His business that I was about. Afterwards, I found the whole thing well performed. And so it is the same in the kitchen (a place to which I have a great natural aversion). I have accustomed myself to doing everything there for the love of God. On all occasions, with prayer, I have found [my work] easy during the fifteen years in which I have been employed here.[3]

Clearly, Nicholas was a man who managed to find God in the kitchen. Scraps of his journals and letters, along with records of a handful of conversations he had with other members of the monastery, were assembled into a short book by one of the monks shortly after his death. Nicholas Herman is better known to us today by the name he took upon entering the service of the monastery: Lawrence of the Resurrection, or, as he was commonly called, Brother Lawrence. The book of his compiled thoughts is called *The Practice of the Presence of God*—a devotional work that

---

2   Brother Lawrence and Frank Laubach, *Practicing His Presence* (Goleta, CA: Christian Books, 1973), 47.
3   Brother Lawrence, *Practicing His Presence*, 47.

has inspired millions of believers over the four centuries since it was written, being published in over 560 different editions and translations.[4] Clearly Brother Lawrence has spoken to a profound human need: finding meaning in the kitchens of ordinary life.

For most of us, the work of a Brother Lawrence is a more relevant example than the martyrdom of a Saint Lawrence. But even so, there is something in my heart that resists wholeheartedly embracing his example. It is not that Brother Lawrence doesn't inspire me—he does. The problem is that I usually think of him as a master of the spiritual life, not a model of a faithful cook. The fact is, I don't want to think of him as a faithful cook because I don't want to think of myself as a faithful cook. Who wants to be *just* a cook or *just* a teacher or *just* a landscaper? I'd much rather be a master of the spiritual life. But God actually called him to be a cook. He wasn't even called to be a famous cook. He was just a cook. He never wrote a book—it was written and compiled by others. Brother Lawrence himself lived and died in his kitchen. Later generations might elect him to the Devotional Hall of Fame, but that was never on his mind at the time—he was just doing the dishes.

Thomas Merton, a modern day monastic and devotional author, offers helpful insight into the conflicted attitudes of those of us who find ourselves working in a less than inspiring job when he writes,

The value of our activity depends almost entirely on the humility to accept ourselves as we are. The reason why we do things so

4 "The Practice of the Presence of God Editions," Goodreads, accessed December 14, 2021, https://www.goodreads.com/.

badly is that we are not content to do what we can. We insist on doing what is not asked of us, because we want to taste the success that belongs to somebody else. We never discover what it is like to make a success of our own work, because we do not want to undertake any work that is merely proportionate to our power. Who is willing to be satisfied with a job that expresses all his limitations? He will accept such work only as "means of livelihood" while he waits to discover his "true vocation." The world is full of unsuccessful businessmen who still secretly believe they were meant to be artists or writers or actors in the movies.[5]

It is hard for many of us to accept that God might give us an ordinary calling, and even harder to admit that such a thing might be proportional to our powers and appropriately reflect our limitations. Another force is often at work as well—we feel guilty about our ordinary life. An ordinary life can be so easy and natural and comfortable that it doesn't seem quite right. Many of us, myself included, have a deep sense that we should aspire to something grand, demanding, challenging, or inspiring. It is not that I want to be martyred, but I do want to be radical. I want to be completely sold out for Jesus. I'm inspired by the quote from Teddy Roosevelt's 1899 speech: "Far better it is to dare mighty things, to win glorious triumphs, even though chequered by failure, than to take rank with those poor souls who neither enjoy much nor suffer much, because they live in the grey twilight that knows neither victory nor defeat."[6] Yet, for all the inspiration this quote brings me, it also makes me cringe. I fear that I will rank among

5   Thomas Merton, *No Man Is an Island* (London: Harcourt, 1983), 124.
6   Theodore Roosevelt, *The Strenuous Life* (n.p.: Vigeo, 2017), 2.

the poor and average souls who live in a grey twilight devoid of both victory and defeat. Strangely enough, I feel guilty before God even though the quote comes from Teddy Roosevelt. I assume that God would never call me to an ordinary life, and that since my life seems pretty ordinary, I must have missed God's calling.

It is at this point that Brother Lawrence is such a good corrective. He sanctified his kitchen and his kitchen sanctified him because he intentionally made Jesus present in everything he did. It was exactly because he embraced his *ordinary* calling as a *divine* calling that he was able to live his life so completely for the sake of Jesus. He was sold out for Jesus so, strangely enough, it didn't really matter what he did. All that mattered was who he did it for. It is exactly this idea that the German theologian and martyr Dietrich Bonhoeffer expresses when he writes about the call of Levi in the Gospels. In his words,

> What does the text inform us about the content of discipleship? Follow me, run along behind me! That is all . . . it gives us no intelligible programme for a way of life, no goal or ideal to strive after. . . . It is nothing else than bondage to Jesus Christ alone, completely breaking through every programme, every ideal, every set of laws. No other significance is possible, since Jesus is the only significance. Beside Jesus nothing has any significance. He alone matters. When we are called to follow Christ, we are summoned to an exclusive attachment to his person.[7]

It is futile to feel guilty about a set of mundane times, places, and circumstances that are not of our own choosing. Such guilt

---

7   Dietrich Bonhoeffer, *The Cost of Discipleship* (New York: Macmillan, 1978), 62–63.

is destructive to our souls. It saps us of our zeal and dims our vision of what faithfulness might look like in the here and now. Jesus put us where we are; we need to embrace our time and place as a gift from him and a divine appointment. If we have refused to follow his voice at some point, then by all means we should repent. If not, we should fully devote ourselves to him right where we are. We should work as "servants of Christ, doing the will of God from the heart, rendering service with a good will as to the Lord and not to man" (Eph. 6:6–7).

### Being a Follower after Christ's Own Heart

What does it mean, then, to be a wholehearted follower of Christ in our ordinary daily lives? What does Jesus really want of us? What does a sold-out life for Christ look like when it doesn't look like a martyr?

The best way to answer this question is by looking at Jesus's own words. One of his favorite teaching motifs was to offer parables about masters and servants. In these parables one is constantly meeting a follower (the servant) who is giving an account of himself to a leader (the master). At the end of the parable, the follower is judged by the master. It is a bit like a gladiator getting a thumbs up or a thumbs down from the emperor. The judgment usually includes an explicit statement of what the servant did well or poorly. It is a great way to form a picture of character qualities, virtues, and practices that constitute faithful following in Jesus's mind. Regardless of the particular tasks a servant is doing in the parable, which vary widely, the good servants always exhibit the sort of following that pleases their master.

When studying these parables, it is easy to underestimate the difficulty of faithful following. This struck me (Rick) a few weeks ago when I found myself singing "I Have Decided to Follow Jesus" in our Sunday morning worship service. The song has its origins in the story of a North Indian martyr in the late ninteenth century. Again, the martyr theme is associated with faithful following here. But as I thought about the words of this song more deeply, I realized that it applies to a lot more than just the life of a martyr. I'm thinking of the haunting and challenging refrain: "still I will follow; no turning back, no turning back."[8] I realized that this phrase fits remarkably well with so many of the characteristics of good followers that emerge from a study of Jesus's parables. In all of these stories there is a servant who has a good reason to either stop following or refuse to start. The key figures in these stories are not merely followers, they are "followers in spite of" or "followers nonetheless." There is a test for each, and each has to say, "Despite this test, still I will follow." Let's dig a little deeper into these parables and consider the tests the servants faced, the service they chose to offer, and the response they received from their master.

## Though Others Tire, Still I Will Follow

In Luke 12:35–40, Jesus begins a set of parables about servants who do and do not please their master. He opens with a group of servants who are to keep the home fires burning while their master is at his wedding feast. The master wants everything ready for his bride upon returning home, and as the night wears on, the

---

8  "I Have Decided to Follow Jesus," accessed December 14, 2021, https://library.timeless truths.org/.

good servants show themselves by their diligence and watchfulness in the late hours. The clear implication is that bad servants do the opposite—they fail their test because they've fallen asleep and aren't ready when the master arrives. Thus, the faithfulness Jesus commends is unflagging readiness and a consistency and determination to stay the course, pressing through challenges without lapsing into negligence or inaction as the hours get later and later into the night.

In the workplace, this quality is found in followers who are always ready for work. They arrive on time, work a full shift, and finish the tasks that are set before them. The task may or may not be difficult. The servants in this particular story are serving as night watchmen at a deserted house rather than master chefs at a wedding feast. They keep the lamps burning and stay dressed for action, but since the parable portrays the feast itself as taking place elsewhere, the main task they ultimately perform is just to open the door when the master knocks. Nonetheless, readiness is demanded, readiness is delivered, and the servants are praised for it.

In this parable, the servants tire in part because of the open-endedness of the future. They just don't know when the bridegroom is coming; they can't look across the plain and track his approaching dust cloud. Instead, they are looking into the darkness and waiting, and wondering, and waiting some more. Oftentimes, we don't tire of working; we tire of waiting.

The Bible offers a different view of the future. The Hebrew word for the future, *aharit*, is a word that literally means "back or behind."[9] This sounds counterintuitive, but Hans W. Wolff

---

9    Edward M. Curtis and John J. Brugaletta, *Discovering the Way of Wisdom: Spirituality in the Wisdom Literature* (Grand Rapids: Kregel Publications, 2004), 125.

offers a helpful analogy of "a rower who moves into the future backwards; he reaches his goal by taking his bearings from what is visibly in front of him."[10] Waiting well as we look into the unknown future requires us to draw encouragement from the long trail of God's faithfulness in our past. His character and faithful deeds provide important reference points for orienting us while we step into an unknown future. In a way, then, we can have a sense that we have been here before. We have waited and found God faithful; we have wondered and found God true; we have wandered but found that he has brought us back. Faithful followers recall God's track record and remember his presence and what he did in revealing just how intimately and purposefully he was involved in our lives. And when we are at a loss for recalling past seasons that resemble a current situation, a trusted friend can often speak into our lives with the wisdom and foresight gained from their own experiences. They may even remind us of life events that have drifted from our recollection.

Of course, the past isn't exclusively a source of encouragement. We can also look back and feel haunted by fear or hunted by enemies. Again, Scripture offers helpful perspective. Psalm 23 describes David walking through the valley of the shadow of death and finding himself in the presence of his enemies. Amid the fear and chaos of encroaching enemies, he is assured with the promise that only God's goodness (*tov*) and covenant love (*hesed*) pursue him (v. 6). David might feel alone, but he is not; he is pursued by God's merciful and loyal love. God is with him. In fact, the very center of this psalm (particularly in the Hebrew

---

10  Hans Walter Wolff, *Anthropology of the Old Testament* (Philadelphia: Fortress Press, 1974), 88.

text) is verse 4, and it includes a distinct shift to address God in second-person language: "Even though I walk through the valley of the shadow of death, I will fear no evil, *for you are with me.*" This great promise can make nights of waiting a little less lonely.

## Though No One Watches, Still I Will Follow

However, Jesus does not stop with mere readiness but develops the parable further in Luke 12:41–48. Here, he offers another image of servants who are given charge over a household, making sure the rest of the servants are properly cared for—a much bigger responsibility. Furthermore, the job is spread over an extended period of time. No longer does the story revolve around a single evening. Instead, the master departs with the intention of being gone for a long time, and the lengthy absence is the reason a servant has to be appointed to manage the household. The master, however, is delayed in returning. The test of the servant, then, is continued faithfulness. Diligence in the midst of a long absence requires a constant readiness for one's work to be inspected (since the time of the master's return is unknown) as well as a refusal to grow negligent though the master's return is much delayed.

These parables, taken together, are really narrative expressions of the command given in Colossians 3:22 for slaves to not only work hard when their master's eye is upon them. The true heart of the servant is shown not in the master's presence but in his absence. It is shown in the seriousness with which the servant takes the master's commands into his own heart and discharges his duties faithfully even if the master is away or delayed in returning. Robert Kelley, in his *Harvard Business Review* article on followership, calls this quality self-management. He notes that "self-managed followers give their organizations a significant cost advantage because they eliminate much of the need for elaborate supervisory control systems."[11] This quality is further manifested in the vigilance required here and in many other places in the New Testament (Matt. 24:36, 42; 25:12; 1 Thess. 5:2; Titus 2:12–13) of those who faithfully follow Christ even if it seems that he tarries in his return. They exhibit an unswerving commitment to do what is required, even when the requirement is not being inspected or enforced at the particular moment. This is not only a quality demanded of faithful followers in the workplace but also of the long, lonely, and seemingly endless service a single mom offers her children. Similar demands are made on a husband whose wife no longer remembers him due to early onset dementia but who nonetheless lovingly feeds her, one spoonful at a time. In all these cases, rewards may one day come, but only after long and lonely hours, days, or decades of serving in the absence of the master.

## Though No One Trains Me, Still I Will Follow

The parables of the talents or minas in Matthew 25:14–30 and Luke 19:12–27 are similar to the previous parables in that the master gives the servants a responsibility and then leaves them to their task. In the case of these parables, however, it seems that the long absence of the master is expected. In other words, the servants in question are not surprised by their master's lengthy absence. They know he is on a long trip, and that affords them an opportunity to demonstrate their own skills as a manager. They are not merely having their perseverance tested but also their

---

11  Robert E. Kelley, "In Praise of Followers," *Harvard Business Review* 66, no. 6 (December 1988): 144.

competency. Will they produce a good return on their investment? No specific instructions are given—they are simply told to do business until he gets home. When he arrives, the master praises those who have done well in terms of their return on investment. The person who had one talent but refused to invest it at all is severely punished. Furthermore, that person's talent is given to the one who already had ten. This seems surprising, but the explanation is that the servant who had proven most competent and most capable was worthy of the reward. Of course, the master entrusted more to this servant because he had proven capable of producing greater results.

This parable tells us how God deals with us, his servants. First, he trusts and entrusts his servants with things of value. Then he tests their industriousness and their competence as stewards. Finally, the master rewards and punishes based on the return on investment. The Lord entrusts the subjects of his kingdom with gifts and graces and he gives his subjects the freedom to use them as they think best. God honors those who are eager to use their talents and gifts for doing good by entrusting them with more. A warning against slothfulness is also given. Those who neglect or squander what God has entrusted to them will lose what they have.

Again, there is an interesting parallel to Kelley's description of an effective follower in the workplace. He calls this quality competence and explains it as follows:

> On the grounds that committed incompetence is still incompetence, effective followers master skills that will be useful to their organizations. They generally hold higher performance standards than the work environment requires, and continuing

education is second nature to them, a staple in their professional development. Less effective followers expect training and development to come to them. The only education they acquire is force-fed. If not sent to a seminar, they don't go. Their competence deteriorates unless some leader gives them parental care and attention.[12]

The effective follower is not forced to be effective but is intrinsically motivated to do well. In contrast, the less effective follower that Kelley describes is almost exactly like the parable's one-talent recipient who refused to deploy his skills or do anything out of his own initiative.

## Though Others Wander, Still I Will Follow

A surprising aspect of Jesus's master-servant parables is that the masters are not always portrayed as being good. Some parables have benevolent, overly generous, or extremely forgiving masters (Luke 15:11–32; Matt. 20:1–16), whereas others have masters with a reputation for being hard, stingy, or even unjust (Luke 18:1–8; 19:21–27; Matt. 25:24–30). It is often unclear if this is an unfair assessment made by the servants—with them merely perceiving the master as hard or unfair even though he really isn't—or if they are accurately identifying the character of the master. But whether the master's faults are real or imagined, the servants' evaluation is never actually disputed in the parables. The parables allow the presumed negative moral character of the master to serve as part of the story. It seems clear, then, that part

---

12 Kelley, "In Praise of Followers," 145.

of the point is that good servants have their own moral compass. They don't just behave well for good masters but also for hard or unfair ones. In all cases, the servant must exercise personal moral judgment whether or not the leader is morally praiseworthy. And, of course, this principle applies equally to the moral failings of a servant. In Luke 12:45, the servant's moral compass goes awry in the absence of his master, and the unfaithful servant drifts into getting drunk and beating the servants he has been put in charge of. The unfaithful servant loses his way, from a moral perspective, once the master's watchful eye is removed, and he is punished accordingly.

What is most vividly clear in all these stories is that faithful followers are not merely passive agents. Their actions, even when performing tasks appointed by their masters, are still their responsibility. No matter the surrounding circumstances, faithful servants know that they will give an account for their behavior. As we mentioned earlier in this book, even if their country is going off the rails or their ministry leader is wandering from biblical morality, followers are still responsible for doing the right thing. They cannot just blame their leaders. They need to exhibit moral stability, moral clarity, and moral courage. Kelley also identifies this quality in his analysis of effective followers when he writes that

> effective followers are credible, honest, and courageous. They establish themselves as independent, critical thinkers whose knowledge and judgment can be trusted. . . . They form their own views and ethical standards and stand up for what they believe in. Insightful, candid, and fearless, they can keep leaders and colleagues honest and informed. The other side of the coin

of course is that they can also cause great trouble for a leader with questionable ethics.[13]

This quality of faithful followers is not just found in a handful of parables but pervades the biblical teaching. In Genesis 3, everyone wants to shift the blame—Adam wants to blame Eve, Eve wants to blame the serpent, and God holds each one accountable for their own actions. Ezekiel 18 reminds us that we are not punished for the misdeeds of others, nor do we gain merit for their good deeds; instead, God promises to judge everyone according to their own ways (Ezek. 18:30). Paul echoes this sentiment when he reminds the church in Rome that each individual will give a personal account to God (Rom. 14:12). Others may wander—in fact, we should expect it—but still we must follow.

## Though No One Praises Me, Still I Will Follow

Our final servant parable speaks to the willingness to do our duty even in the absence of praise or reward. Duty seems to have become a dirty word in recent years. When we talk about duty, which we seldom do, it is almost always with a negative connotation. It is a term used for an unwelcome or onerous obligation that we must perform. When we do our duty, we think we have made some sort of sacrifice, and therefore we feel like we are owed something in return. It is as if we were coerced into doing something and should therefore get a reward to make up for the violation of our free will. But nothing could be further from Jesus's description of duty in Luke 17:7–10.

13  Kelley, "In Praise of Followers," 146.

In what is often called the parable of the unworthy servants, Jesus describes a servant who is tending sheep or working the field and, upon coming into the house, is called on to make dinner rather than recline at the table. The servant only eats once the master has been served. Just to make it worse for our modern tastes, Jesus asks the rhetorical question, "Does he thank the servant because he did what was commanded?" (Luke 17:9). The assumed answer is no—no thanks is expected, required, or given. And at the end, Jesus sums the story up by saying, "So you also, when you have done all that you were commanded, say, 'We are unworthy servants; we have only done what was our duty'" (Luke 17:10).

I will be honest here: I'm not really fond of this parable, but Jesus told it nonetheless. Though there appears to be some tension between this story and many others in which rewards are included, the contrast is less than it seems. The parable of the unworthy servants simply makes the point that our rewards are not obligations owed to us by God but rather acts of divine grace. Our service is an ordinary expectation God has of us; it is not an extraordinary sacrifice that demands repayment. In this parable, Jesus wants to make it clear that we can never put God in our debt. We are compelled to serve God, and because we are compelled, service is merely God's due. We are compelled to serve as a natural duty owed by creature to Creator; we are compelled to serve because of his love for us; we are compelled by his sacrifice for us; we are compelled because he opens his hand and "satisf[ies] the desire of every living thing" (Ps. 145:16).

The point of the parable is that the compulsion just goes one way. To borrow Oswald Chambers's phrase, when I offer "my utmost for his highest," I have simply done my duty.[14] This love-compelled service is manifested through the tenacious work ethic of the faithful follower who serves, even when tired, and doesn't expect a bonus reward for doing so. We are to run with perseverance the race that is set before us (2 Tim. 4:7; Heb. 12:1–3). It is *our* race; who else is supposed to run it? The diligence, perseverance, and endurance we bring to the tasks we perform—whether in the church, the workplace, the family, or the larger community—are really just the fulfillment of our sense of divine calling as a servant to the Master who gave all to us so that we can give our all back to him. This is not a perspective that makes a lot of sense in the secular world. Unlike many of the other qualities we have mentioned, we did not find an example of it in Kelley's discussion of followership. Perhaps that is because living out this quality of faithful followership is dependent on serving a great God, abiding in Christ, attaching ourselves to his vine, being nourished by the presence of the Holy Spirit, and finding the power of God working in our weakness.

## Conclusion

After studying these parables, it is clear that the list of qualities Jesus demands of his followers is daunting. Following is not for the faint of heart. It demands long hours; it may have to be done with little direction; it may require creativity and dedicated service without praise or acknowledgment; it may require the courage to follow one's own moral compass in the face of leadership that seems to have lost its way. Qualities of this sort are not simply

14  Oswald Chambers, *My Utmost for His Highest: The Golden Book of Oswald Chambers* (New York: Dodd, Mead, 1935).

drummed up on the spot. They have to be cultivated. They are not instantaneous decisions but products of a lifetime of choices. As the saying goes, you were born looking like your parents but you die looking like your decisions. The most important decisions we make are usually not the one or two big ones that seem important at the time but rather the thousand tiny ones that ultimately add up to our character.

Therefore, we will now turn our attention to practices we need to do in order to develop such a character. We will call them soul rhythms. And as a word of encouragement, these soul rhythms actually turn out to be nothing more or less than learning to live like Christ—something that he describes as an easy yoke and a light burden. Perhaps counterintuitively, in light of what we have just discussed, it is the only sort of life in which we can find rest for our souls.

7

# Soul Rhythms for
# Faithful Following

*And though the Lord give you the bread of adversity*
*and the water of affliction, yet your Teacher will not*
*hide himself anymore, but your eyes shall see your*
*Teacher. And your ears shall hear a word behind*
*you, saying, "This is the way, walk in it," when you*
*turn to the right or when you turn to the left.*

ISAIAH 30:20–21

IN THE PREVIOUS CHAPTER, we discovered that the virtues required to follow Christ in the midst of our ordinary lives are actually anything but ordinary. In fact, they are quite demanding. At the end of the chapter, however, we assured you that cultivating these virtues is not a tiresome, life-sapping burden but rather the easy yoke that Christ promised to his followers. The high calling of the faithful follower, demanding as it might seem, is actually the key to finding rest for our souls. How is this possible?

For me (Joanne), this is not a philosophical or rhetorical question. It has now been seventeen years and counting that by God's grace my husband Norm has been clean and sober. In the spring of 2004, he entered a recovery clinic for his addiction to cocaine. As I learned in family counseling, a family system is like a child's mobile—pulling one dangling bauble disrupts the entire whole. My whole was disrupted. The bitterness, resentment, disappointment, unforgiveness, and fear that I often felt spiraled in my woundedness. My ordinary life had suddenly become extraordinarily difficult. It was not long afterward, in quiet moments with God, that he began to show me how he had been preparing me ahead of time for this life-changing rollercoaster of a challenge. In the two years prior, he stirred in me a deep interest in knowing my identity in Christ. This became, and still is, a key theme in my classes, but it is also my settling desire for a growing dependence on his Spirit to transform my heart. Soul rhythms became God's pathways toward that end and the lifeblood of our long recovery process. Though triggers and temptations still come, they are fewer and less intense, and I know and see him completing his work in me.

If you follow Christ, the great gift of regeneration through the Holy Spirit means that you actually have a new life. We are new creations in Christ. That is who we truly are. Trying to live any other way is tiring—downright exhausting. Why? Because our inmost heart now beats with the love of God and a desire to walk in his ways (Rom. 6:17). That is why Jesus could promise that his yoke was easy and his burden was light. It may not always feel that way, but that is because we have yet to see Christ fully formed in us. It is also because we have spent years habituating ourselves to act in ways that are contrary to God's ways. We need to transform a mind that up to this point has been conformed to the world.

## Soul Rhythms

The soul rhythms we are about to consider are practices that help Christian transformation reach its full expression. Some may refer to these soul rhythms as spiritual disciplines or devotional practices. It does not matter much what they are called; the name is not the point. In fact, learning to practice these soul rhythms or spiritual disciplines is not even the point. The point is to grow up as a child of God, becoming more like Christ through an acute sensitivity to God's Spirit and a heartfelt willingness to be led by him (Gal. 5:25). We use the word "rhythms" in this context because, like the beat of a song, these practices need to be repeated in order to get the feel of them, and once you have the feel of them they need to be repeated until your soul hears them subconsciously—a bit like a song that is running through the back of your mind. These rhythms are directed at the heart, the place where thoughts, emotions, and will converge, and from which flow the issues of life (Prov. 4:23). Our description of each rhythm ends with a short invitation to try it out in some particular way. In our experience, some people are drawn to certain practices more than others. That's just fine; start with trying what most captures your attention and not worrying about those that don't.

We encourage you to read these invitations as opportunities for personal engagement with God, not merely opportunities for intellectual reflection. Following is deeply relational—it describes a certain sort of posture between two people. And as we have argued throughout this book, following always points us all the way back to Jesus himself. If we desire to be better followers, we are really just wanting to be more closely connected to Jesus himself. This was the lesson Brother Lawrence offered us—for those who are faithful followers, even working in the kitchen is working in the presence of God. Likewise, these exercises are meant to draw us more closely to God and develop rhythms that help us practice the presence of God in our lives. You may find it helpful to reword these invitations as personal invitations from Jesus to you. You might even insert your own name.

The practices associated with life transformation are challenging yet simple. They are simple in that they are universal and timeless biblical rhythms that have been practiced by those who have followed God down through the ages. They are challenging because they require time and attention, two of the most irreplaceable and treasured commodities in our restless, speed-immersed, caffeine-saturated, sleep-deprived, entertainment-entitled, inbox-addicted, notifications-assaulted, meetings-overloaded, relationship-starved lives. We're not going to sugarcoat this. Dedicated intention and time is essential for any of these rhythms to become a lifestyle and for our lifestyles to bear evidence of transformation. But on the other hand, refusing to adopt these rhythms is far more exhausting because it leaves us caught in the whirlwind of contemporary culture and also leaves us at odds with our very heart—the new heart we received when we were made alive again in Christ. Our new nature demands expression, and true rest will only be found as we learn to live according to the rhythms that our new heart demands. The evil one thrives on disrupting and sabotaging our intentions to live into our transformed heart. One of the best ways for him to do this is simply to keep us from making the serious attempt to train our lives according to these rhythms. This point is nicely stated in a poster I saw recently, which read, "We don't rise to the level of our expectations; we fall to the level of our training."

But the good news is that we are not alone. It is not primarily our work at all. It is a joint effort wherein we choose to answer his call but only succeed because of the work of his Spirit. God's Spirit acts as a direct agent in our transformation, applying what we know to our growth in Christlikeness (1 Cor. 6:11; 2 Thess. 2:13).

## Knowing the God of the Word through the Word of God

The most foundational soul rhythm is learning to know God. This begins with realizing that God desires to be known. As the prophet Jeremiah recorded,

> Thus says the LORD: "Let not the wise man boast in his wisdom, let not the mighty man boast in his might, let not the rich man boast in his riches, *but let him who boasts boast in this, that he understands and knows me,* that I am the LORD who practices steadfast love, justice, and righteousness in the earth. For *in these things I delight, declares the* LORD." (Jer. 9:23–24)

God delights in us when we know and understand him. It is what we were made for. But God dwells in unapproachable light—no one can see or know him unless he chooses to reveal himself to us. Of course, God's greatest act of revelation was to send Jesus, the living Word. But we do not live in ancient Palestine, so today, we know Jesus best through his written word as illuminated and applied by his Holy Spirit.

It seems natural, then, to say that the way we are supposed to know God is through knowing his word. This is true enough, but for many of us, something goes awry. The issue turns on *how* we read the Bible, not *how much* or *how often*. Perhaps an analogy would help. Imagine you are married but your spouse is travelling for an extended period of time in another country. Because you cannot see each other face-to-face, you write letters to each other. Of course, you are delighted when a new letter arrives and you read it eagerly. You probably even go back and reread old letters. The letters include your thoughts and feelings about each other, but a large portion of these letters just describe what is going on in your daily lives. Yet all of your writing and reading is for a very clear purpose: you want to stay connected and know what's going on in each other's lives. You are not really writing *love* letters; you are writing *life* letters. The same is true of Scripture—it is a life letter to us from God. We need to read it that way. It contains many direct statements about God himself (his being and nature), but a lot of how God makes himself known is by sharing his perspective of, concerns about, and commands for daily life. Reading Scripture as a life letter has two simultaneous and related benefits: it helps us live our lives better, and it also helps us know God better.

Here's how this has worked for me (Joanne). Part of my routine of getting ready and being readied for the day is by spending time with God in the morning just after waking up. Sometimes I would rather keep pushing the snooze button than get up, go to my desk, open my Bible and journal, and sit with him. Surely he understands how tired I am and how much I could use more rest, I argue (or whine). Yet, I know he has something for me.

That simple thought, "God has something for me," is often the difference between rising to hear his voice and hitting the snooze button. I get up and head in the right direction. And guess what? He always has something for me—it may be about himself, it may be about his perspective on my life, it may be about the lives of others I know and love, but he always has something for me. And whatever he has always helps me know him better. Reading the Bible does that—it reveals more of who he is in the reality of being all-powerful, all-knowing, all-good, and ever-present. Beyond space and time, in the here and now, I am graced with his presence. As we converse, he shows me that he really does know what he's talking about—not just about himself but also about my life. Knowing him, and knowing he knows me, also leads me to trust him more. It's difficult to trust someone you do not know.

However, it hasn't always been like this. Over the years, I have at times fallen out of reading the Bible with a posture that fosters the readiness and moment-by-moment dependence on the Lord that is needed for genuine transformation. I still have a sense of loss about these times. Save yourself some time, turmoil, and regrets by adopting some healthy postures toward reading the word:

- Be willing to savor a candlelight meal of God's word, the bread of life, rather than eat it like fast-food (rushed and while driving) or a nutritional supplement (which is quick, easy, and mechanical).
- Be willing to daily feed on God's word. (Welcome his precepts that nourish the whole of life, and don't just read the Bible in times of crisis. God's word is not a magical cure for the ills of a particular moment; it is meant to be our daily bread.)

- Be willing to hear what you don't want to hear about God. (He is a God of justice, holiness, and righteousness, and he is also a God of wrath. Be open to know what he loves and what he hates. We are not judged by whether or not we are true to ourselves; we are judged by whether or not we have been true to him and genuinely followed him as our Lord and Savior)
- Be willing to hear what you don't want to hear about yourself. (God's word is wielded by the Spirit and designed to uncover the suppressed realities of a prideful heart. You are not having a passive quiet time; you are going in for heart surgery.)
- Be open to the Holy Spirit's illumination of God's word and his leading you toward obedience, integrity, and transformation. (Begin your study by imagining yourself stepping onto his altar as a living sacrifice. Your knowledge of him will culminate in actions that reflect him.)

As I get to know God through his word, I become more attentive and less dismissive, more engaged and less distant, more alert and less deaf to his voice, more conversant with him and less oblivious. I follow more closely rather than go my own way. I know my purpose with greater clarity and am affirmed of his abiding presence.

---

*You are invited . . .*
*. . . to quiet your soul, read God's word, and make room for his Spirit to show you an important life challenge through his eyes.*

---

## Reading to Align with the Holy Spirit

Gordon MacDonald reminds us that

> character is developed when we let the Scripture inform us. We are what we permit to enter the deepest part of our soul. A steady diet of television, cheap publications, and shallow literature will make us dreadfully inadequate people. A daily exposure to the Scripture and to literature that focuses on Scripture is a necessary part of the diet.[1]

We were never designed to be "dreadfully inadequate people." God's Spirit works in us for our flourishing. He works in concert with God's word. He teaches believers all things (John 14:26) and guides us into all truth (John 16:13). Therefore, a growing knowledge of God's will requires greater engagement with his Spirit. God's Spirit knows the mind of God (1 Cor. 2:11) and how to best accomplish what God wants done. As God's divine agent, his Spirit directs, assures, and affirms our steps along the path he has set before us.

The psalmist reminds the faithful follower that every day of every human life is written in God's book and planned before a single day comes to pass (Ps. 139:16). What an incredible encouragement and relief to those who are anxiously seeking his ways. God already knows the joys and sorrows, victories and failures, calamities, doubts, challenges, and temptations we currently experience and will experience. We can echo this in conversations with God: "Okay, Lord, I feel worried, but

---

1   Gordon MacDonald, *A Resilient Life* (Nashville: Thomas Nelson, 2004), 65.

you knew this was going to happen. With the grace and power of your Spirit, how do you want me to respond?" As the Spirit works in concert with the Scriptures to ensure that God's will is accomplished in a manner that reflects his character, we are invited to recognize God's presence and to cooperate with him. We discover that in God's presence we find joy (Ps. 16:11), wisdom (Prov. 17:24), rest (Ex. 33:14; Matt. 11:28–29), and protection (Ps. 31:20)—all of which help us move from a place of anxious wondering about where we are heading to a place of restful assurance that we are in his will. The Spirit provides all that is needed to follow well.

---

*You are invited . . .*
*. . . to follow God's Spirit in a situation where you have been resistant to his lead.*

---

## Allowing God's Word to Penetrate the Heart

For the truths of Scripture to have their desired effect, they must not merely be read—they must also penetrate deeply into our hearts. The soul rhythm that facilitates this is biblical meditation. The English Puritans sometimes referred to biblical meditation as "conferencing with ourselves," that is, talking to ourselves about spiritual things. We can conference in our personal study of God's word as we ask questions, seek answers, and allow the truth of the Scriptures to sink deeply into our hearts.[2] Conferencing (or meditation) gives an opportunity for God to knead the truth of

2  "How Can We Develop Deep Relationships in a Surface-Level Culture?" *Biola Magazine*, October 22, 2018, https://www.biola.edu/.

his word into the dough of our souls. It allows us to see his truths as a spiritual plumb line for our lives and bring perspective and wisdom to our thinking, situations, and actions.

In my own times of conference with God, he often impresses on my soul the need to refrain from an action or repent of one. Sometimes God wisely corrects an attitude and thus greatly improves subsequent interactions and conversations. My seasons of conference have had tremendous benefits for my conversations with family members, friends, colleagues, students, and leaders. It has deepened my desire for the Spirit to direct my spoken words in order to better reflect the character of God. It has also given me the freedom to speak more boldly—knowing that God has given me words that will be truthful, gracious, and kind—and allowed me to have far fewer regrets, even as years pass and the specifics of these conversations are long forgotten.

The Puritans viewed conferencing with oneself as part of a larger whole. They also valued conferencing with others but still for the same purpose of aligning our personal lives with God's truths. Exercised in pairs, families, and small groups, the practice of conferencing brought believers together in honest and transparent dialogue centered around scriptural truths drawn from private Bible reading or notes taken from sermons. English Puritan Thomas Shepard instructed believers to "put . . . questions to others, sometimes to teach, and sometimes to be taught; and this do, if possible, in all occasional meetings, and worldly discourses; mix with it sweet truth that God has taught thee."[3] The gentle, genuine, conversational exchange of thoughts infused the

---

3   Thomas Shepard, *Subjection to Christ in All His Ordinances* (London: Printed for John Rothell, 1652), 51.

hearts of all participants with godly perspectives on the challenges facing their daily lives.

Today, many have had accountability partners and benefitted from them, yet accountability groups are often built around a regular set of questions or some other set structure. Human beings are good at being deceitful and duplicitous, and it is particularly easy to be this way when you know exactly what questions are coming ahead of time. Conferencing, as the Puritans conceived it, was a more open-ended conversation allowing another person to be attentive to the issues of the heart, not all of which were explicitly spoken. This attention to the heart extended to the good, bad, and ugly—prideful motives, failures in thought, weaknesses in temptations, duplicity in challenges, spin on matters, doubts in trials, celebrations and victories both big and small, and growth in gratitude, humility, and godliness. There are risks involved with this level of attentiveness, but it is riskier still to leave the corners of our hearts unexplored and neglected.

Godly conference promotes an awareness and alertness to God's movements in and through life circumstances. God's actions are infinitely precise and, with the help of others, we can see that precision more clearly. Conference with others helps us become increasingly alert to the intersections of the divine and temporal, the visible and the invisible; it also helps us see God's hand acting in ways that we might otherwise miss.

---

*You are invited . . .*
*. . . to conference with God or a trusted friend, attending to them with your whole heart, even as they attend to you.*

---

## Listening in Silence and Solitude

We have grown accustomed to noise. Whether it's background music, white noise, or sounds from any of our devices, it is our constant companion wherever we travel, rest, work, or think. We are so accustomed to the noise that we often feel reluctant to turn off a device when it's time for a meal or when a guest arrives. Control has been forfeited to our devices more than we recognize or care to admit. But soul rhythms of silence and solitude push back against this tendency. In many ways, both silence and solitude are forms of fasting. Though fasting is usually associated with food, one can readily see how silence might be considered a form of fasting from noise. Likewise, solitude is a form of fasting from sociality, whether we are physically alone or simply separating ourselves from the constant onslaught of social media. Silence and solitude create space to see the contents of our hearts, to reassert the control we actually have, and to recover our misplaced dependencies on other people and things.

The combination of these soul rhythms is natural. They complement each other in practice and outcome. In silence and solitude we bring our fears and idols, our truest motivations, and our most cunning deceptions before the face of God. It can be scary. Sin made Adam and Eve want to hide from God's presence, and our sin does the same to us—all of our noise and the clutter of our activities are like hiding places from the presence of God. But solitude and silence can strip these hiding places away and allow us—force us, really—to stand before God.

When I (Joanne) humbly take the time to be in the presence of God for the sole purpose of self-reflection and allowing his voice of truth to address my misplaced allegiances, I have found that

God is surprisingly gentle in addressing my fears and dethroning my idols. And though nothing surprises him, he often surprises me with the immediacy of his unfailing grace, forgiveness, and restoration. This is freedom.

I have also found that along with slowing my busyness and recovering my energy, it is not uncommon for the free space created by silence and solitude to become the source of innovative solutions to problems I am facing. In this time and space, I gain a broader perspective of matters and am more able to allow creative ideas to germinate. It is not uncommon for God to allow me to see connections between matters I thought were unrelated, which also opens up ideas for new responses.

One's investment in the practice of silence and solitude can last a few hours, days, or weeks, but it can also be effective in surprisingly short periods of time. Standing in a longer line at the market and using that time to ask for God's perspective or to bring a pressing matter before him helps cultivate a familiarity of recognizing his presence. I confess I have sometimes had a well-meaning cashier tug at my cart and invite me to an open register that had no line. My decline of the offer and my explanation that I was perfectly fine with the longer wait was met with a greater insistence and stronger tug on my cart. In a world that is aflame with hurry, it is hard to imagine a person voluntarily waiting. Nonetheless, I simply smile and say, "No, thank you," and then resume my time with Jesus.

Further, knowing ourselves more fully may move us to express this same honesty and vulnerability to others. Experiencing the Spirit speaking in our own lives can guide us in how to speak to others—and also to know when no words need to be spoken at all.

In our growing comfort with silence, we also no longer sense the urge to say something (anything!) to break the felt awkwardness of silence. This graciously affords others more time to consider their own thoughts and words. Words that are shared become more meaningful and our perspectives become more others-centered. And words that are delayed or unspoken also give room for God to speak to others—oftentimes with words far more effective than we could ever muster on our own.

Part of my (Joanne's) responsibilities in overseeing online education at Talbot School of Theology is to support faculty in offering quality education in an online format. After reviewing a slate of surveys for one of our professors, I scheduled a time with him to address the low-scoring student evaluations and comments. Conventional wisdom would suggest I needed to take the initiative and know exactly what to say—perhaps a clear message like "shape up or ship out." Having set aside some time beforehand to hear from God, however, I started with a word of gratitude for serving our students. I acknowledged his passion for the subject he was teaching and his ability to communicate well. In acknowledging that I had reviewed the survey results, I mentioned my suspicion that he probably had ideas for how he would improve his engagement with the students and his own teaching effectiveness. I asked if he would share them with me. The ideas he had were wonderful and also fell within the parameters of effective pedagogy, so I gave him permission to execute them the very next semester. The survey results at the end of that semester were remarkable. What a difference! Not only did the student learning experience improve drastically but the professor's experience set him on a better trajectory for years to come. In a follow-up conversation, we both shared the delight in how effective his ideas were and how grateful I was for his involvement and investment with our students. The conversation and results would probably have been quite different had we gone the typical route of focusing on the poor scores. I'm grateful I listened to the Spirit before speaking!

---

*You are invited . . .*

*. . . to embrace a moment of silence with God in which you might otherwise have spoken.*

---

## Prayer

Communion with God through the soul rhythm of prayer is that sacred time and space where we are welcomed into the presence of the Creator of the universe who is at the same time our perfect Father. When asked, though, most people (even Christians) admit that they exercise prayer primarily to ask for something. Jesus instructs his followers to ask him for things, so it certainly is not wrong to do so. Yet, when this becomes the primary way we pray, we lose sight of who God is, our relationship with him, and the purpose of prayer. Our disappointment with his answers lead us to believe he is powerless or disinterested in our lives, so we pray less.

Allowing God's word to guide our prayer life can reshape our conversations with him. It is as important to hear from God in prayer as it is to speak with him. With a growing knowledge of God through his word and an increasing sensitivity to the Spirit as he applies that word to our hearts, we often find the focus of our prayers changing as God reveals the need for restoring a relationship, strengthens our character and integrity, or gives unexpected guidance for matters that we didn't even know we needed help with. The more we understand and exercise the grace and power of prayer, the more clearly and frequently we'll see God's movements. Greater acknowledgment fuels the desire to pray more and to pray with greater specificity and anticipation.

Our conversations with God need not be eloquent in order to gain his attention to our prayers. Young children often bring their own paintings home from school. Though not a Picasso or Monet, that artwork is prominently displayed on a wall or refrigerator door with great pride and pleasure for all to see. Why? Not because the artwork is a masterpiece but because of who the artist is and the relationship that child has with a parent or guardian. Similarly, God delights in hearing the words, whispers, sighs, and cries of our prayers because of who he is and who we are in relationship to him.

And he welcomes prayers that do not look or sound like anything we would assume to be a prayer. This is particularly true with prayers of lament, when we cry out in our humanness at the injustices, devastations, and turmoil we suffer. Our messiness will never bar us from the welcome and grace of God. He is familiar with tears, anger, death; he knows the sin we inflict on ourselves and others. Sometimes, we simply do not have the words to utter to God. Sometimes we wail. Sometimes in our despair we throw our fists up to him. And sometimes our words are few. He is great enough to know and understand our finitude and inabilities, and he welcomes all these faltering efforts at prayer.

A few words of caution are needed here with regard to prayer. When we feel pressed to hear an immediate answer from God but no answer comes, we sometimes choose to forge ahead because, we reason, "I didn't hear God say no!" But genuine prayer is often a waiting prayer. Delayed or ambiguous answers to prayer can actually become strategic pauses amid the flurry of emotion-fueled demands that allow a person to regain moment-by-moment alertness to the leading of the Spirit. The absence of a clear sense of direction may actually be directing us back to God himself who is calling us to simply wait and be in his presence. God may still be working on details and matters beyond our own comprehension, and your participation in bringing about his intended outcome may be jeopardized by an impatient reaction or abrupt decision.

*You are invited . . .*
*. . . to pause and hear God, even as he hears you.*

## Humility

Humility is one of the most striking and important character traits exhibited by the incarnate Christ—we should never understand it as merely being a doormat for others. The fundamental meaning of the Greek word for humble is simply to be low or under. Jesus's life and completed work on the cross models this kind of humility, exemplifying his submission to the Father and complete devotion to and dependence on him. This aspect of Jesus's life was discussed at length in chapter 3. By virtue of the union we have with him (i.e., being "in Christ"), we share the humility of his crucifixion (Gal. 2:20; Rom. 6:2–6). The natural heart, which is "deceitful above all things, and desperately sick" (Jer. 17:9), is far removed from Jesus's kind of humility. In order to align with Jesus's heart, our hearts need to be broken. Humility is required to recognize Jesus's power and authority in our lives and to listen and respond in submission and obedience to him. It takes Spirit-empowered humility to live responsively as a faithful follower and selfless servant. There is a unifying strength and freedom in humility and it is developed in, through, and for the community.

## Humility and the Grace of Confession

One way to form Christlike humility in our lives is through confession. It is only in this practice that the path to freedom and wholeness is opened. Almost everything about human anatomy is directed forward: eyes, ears, nose, mouth, elbows, hands, knees, and feet. Spiritually, God's design is for human beings to move forward as well. Yet unconfessed sin is like an anchor behind us. It ties us to a past that we cannot yet leave behind. Without confession and complete forgiveness, forward movement eludes us. We rationalize—or, more accurately, we tell ourselves "rational lies"—by playing the victim or shifting blame to others. Knowing the human heart and what hinders and prevents our forward movement, God provides all that is needed for a renewed and restored direction through Jesus's work on the cross and the grace of confession.

Confession is humbling because it confronts us with our authentic self—no spin or pretense. In confession, image management that seeks to please others gives way to image bearing—we know we are made to bear the image of a holy God, and to harbor sin tarnishes that image. Faithful followers confess. They own up; they come clean. The grace of confession is the avenue by which complete forgiveness is received and actualized in repentance, a re-turning ourselves to Jesus and his ways. We face the unconfessed sin that distorts who we are and hides the reality of who God has made us to be. Our lives become less compartmentalized. Our private self, public self, blind spots, and even our unconscious self increasingly become one. When confession, repentance, and complete forgiveness are experienced, we really only need one self—fallen but restored, needy but filled with grace, guilty but forgiven—and since that self is free to stand unashamed before God's throne in the holy of holies, it has nothing to fear from any human being.

---

*You are invited . . .*
*. . . to let God help you cut the rope that has bound you to a past that needs to be left behind.*

---

### Humility and the Grace of Giving Thanks

The gratitude that often follows confession in prayer is typically expressions of thankfulness for blessings received. Perhaps the proper initial response to confession is the grateful recognition of what it cost God to offer complete forgiveness: Christ's finished work on the cross. It is the proper response to having received God's grace (2 Cor. 4:15). In fact, grace and gratitude are semantically related: grace (*charis*) is God's undeserved favor toward us, but it is also the gratitude (*eucharisteō*) we give in response to God's favor. For the blessings of an ever-available restoration to wholeness in our relationship with God and the promise of abundant life in him, we give thanks.

Thanksgiving serves as a barometer of growth in Christlikeness. Paul assumes our normal condition to be so full of grace that we always overflow with thanks. He even commands us to give thanks—a command that would be impossible to obey if grace was not constantly being poured out upon us (Eph. 5:20; Col. 3:15–17). With respect to God, giving thanks is a recognition of the favor he shows us in his countless acts on our behalf that we could never do for ourselves. Since thanks is associated with something one couldn't have done for oneself, giving thanks usually involves acknowledging one's own weaknesses, needs, or failures. This requires humility—especially when thanksgiving is expressed publicly—which means that gratitude is an antidote to our hidden pride. Among the symptoms of ingratitude is a distancing from others and a distancing from God. Ingratitude thwarts empathy and trust, and the more we refrain from giving thanks, the more we recoil from relational engagement. We slowly learn to shun opportunities to sit face-to-face with other human beings, made in God's image, who may desperately need a simple word of affirmation, grace, or gratitude. When we experience a lack of affirmation or grace, we become reluctant to express gratitude. An effective way to break this cycle is the soul rhythm of gratitude, heartfelt thanksgiving that is expressed to others. Have you ever noticed the surprise on someone's face when an unexpected thank-you is spoken to an unsuspecting custodian, groundskeeper, or grocery worker?

When we distance ourselves from God, our communication with God through prayer becomes anemic. We pray without enthusiasm or expectation. Our vague requests blind us from seeing his undeniable answers or we chalk his answers off as fate.

Perceived unanswered prayers fuel discouragement, disappointment, and ingratitude. Thanklessness is embedded in pride and self-sufficiency and thus is a major roadblock to an intimate life with God. We fail to recognize what has been given and the one who gives. We forget Paul's humilty-cultivating question, "What do you have that you did not receive?" (1 Cor. 4:7).

Our thanksgiving can also be curtailed by the things that we actually do receive that are unpleasant, difficult, or even hurtful. Unwelcome events test our theology. Do we believe that God is actively working for our good? One of the themes of the New Testament is that God gives good gifts (Matt. 7:11)—in fact, he is the source of all good gifts (James 1:17)—and that he works all things together for the good if we are called according to his purpose (Rom. 8:28). God's gifts may not always look good at the outset, but they are given to help conform us to the image of his Son (Rom. 8:29). His gift may look like a thorn in our flesh, but he gives it to us to help us discover the sufficiency of his grace and a power that is not our own (2 Cor. 12:9). One might say that God is great at giving gifts, but we might not like the way they are wrapped. Choosing to unwrap our life experiences with humble gratitude is a challenging but extremely important spiritual rhythm.

No matter the circumstances, faithful followers respond to the grace that God extends to us through Christ with gratitude to him and gratitude to others, our fellow recipients and stewards of his kindness. The benefits of giving thanks are well-documented in promoting mental, emotional, and physical wellness. As antidotes to pride, expressions of gratitude also serve to counter loneliness, alleviate imposter syndrome, and reduce levels of stress. Further, gratitude diminishes overinflated desires for material goods. It can help make us more patient with others because we have trained our eyes and hearts to see the many good things they offer. It can deepen friendships by helping us savor and express the joys our friends bring to us. And, finally, gratitude helps us find meaning in our work by recognizing the good embedded in the activities we do.

---

*You are invited . . .*

*. . . to cultivate the heart and words of gratitude for a person, event, or strangely wrapped gift that has been difficult to accept as coming from God.*

---

## Hospitality to the Stranger, the Would-Be Friend

The word "hospitality" may bring to mind images of lavish dinner tables overflowing with food or possibly the hospitality industry, which meets the lodging and food needs of travelers or special events. But God sees hospitality differently, and the difference stems from the importance he places on relationships.

God commands his followers to be hospitable, a term that literally means "to love strangers." The spirit of hospitality is an attitude of selflessness that is characterized by the extension of friendship to a stranger. Biblical hospitality crosses social barriers of race, ethnicity, culture, class, and economic status—anything that distinguishes individuals—and it also counters the pervasive practice of "othering." At its most basic level, "othering" can be the divisive language of "us versus them"—language that tends to polarize, exclude, and objectify other people. If allowed free rein, it actually serves to dehumanize those made in the image of God. Extending friendship to a stranger without expectation of reciprocity, exchange, or leveraging is a testimony to the outworking of God's Spirit. Such freely given welcome shines brightly in a culture of "me, myself, and I" and closes the gap between insiders and outsiders of any kind.

Here's a good example of the non-elaborate, non-industry vision of hospitality to which God calls us. Anne, a cashier at the market where I (Joanne) shop, doesn't look like me. She is a recovering alcoholic, celebrating almost four years of being clean and sober. Over time, our simple contact through shopping has opened a door to hospitality. We have become friends. I bring her freshly baked zucchini bread, and she in turn has brought me homemade tamales and navy bean soup. The other day after I paid for my groceries, she told me she was glad I came in. It had been a tough day for her. Her words were not just a casual comment—they were an opportunity to practice hospitality. So right there in line, I leaned in toward her and prayed for her. I just now received a text message from her inviting me over for lunch. Our relationship started with something as small as me calling her by name and acknowledging her gift for humor. No fancy dinners were required!

The friendship of and with God brings redemption and salvation. Paul states in Ephesians 2:18–19 that through Christ, "we both [Jew and Gentile] have access in one Spirit to the Father. So then you are no longer strangers and aliens, but you are fellow citizens with the saints and members of the household of God." It is remarkable to note that God's great gift of salvation was also a gift of hospitality. Not only has salvation brought us out of darkness into God's glorious light, it has also welcomed strangers into the household of God and torn down a dividing wall of hostility (Eph. 2:14). Extending friendship to a stranger serves as a reflection of what God has done for us when we were strangers. We need only remember how God did this for us and how he will empower us to imitate him by welcoming others. Generous friendship to strangers becomes characteristic of tenacious followers. The ever-widening impact on cultivating and enlarging the community is unquestionable.

---

*You are invited . . .*

*. . . to extend friendship to a previously unseen or neglected stranger.*

---

## Conclusion

The soul rhythms and invitations above are designed to kindle one's sensitivity to and deepen one's conversation with the Spirit. It is he who leads as we follow in the ordinariness of life's circumstances and relationships. As those who are united to Christ and live in Christ, we are given the privilege and responsibility to represent him to others 24-7. In 2 Corinthians 5:20, Paul writes, "Therefore, we are ambassadors for Christ, God making his appeal through us. We implore you on behalf of Christ, be reconciled to God." Though translated as a noun here, the Greek word used for "ambassador" is a verb; we are ambassador-ing on behalf of Christ.[4] As ambassadors, God is sending us not just as

---

4    Kenneth Berding, *How to Live An "In Christ" Life: 100 Devotional Readings on Union with Christ* ([Fearn, Ross-shire, Scotland?]: Christian Focus Publications, 2020), 208.

his representatives but also as his conduits. We are the way God shares himself with others:

- We love because he first loved us (1 John 4:19).
- We forgive because he first forgave us (Col. 3:13).
- We comfort with the comfort he gives us (2 Cor. 1:3–4).
- We serve because he came to serve (Mark 10:45; Matt. 20:28).
- We give because we have freely received (Matt. 10:8).
- We extend mercy because he is merciful to us (Matt. 18:33).
- We reconcile with others because he reconciled himself to us (2 Cor. 5:18).
- We welcome because he first welcomed us (Rom. 15:7).

From his abundance, Jesus freely gives so that you and I might be open conduits of what we have freely and humbly received. Faithful followers depend on the Spirit's lead as they extend love, forgiveness, comfort, and friendship to those in today's hurting world. He directs us to the very ones who are in need of God's graces, be they family, friend, acquaintance, or stranger.

---

*You are invited . . .*
*. . . to be God's ambassador—to give from the abundance you have already received.*

---

8

# The Rewards of Following

*If we consider the unblushing promises of reward
and the staggering nature of the rewards promised
in the Gospels, it would seem that Our Lord
finds our desires not too strong, but too weak.*

C. S. LEWIS, *THE WEIGHT OF GLORY*

C. S. LEWIS FIRST SPOKE THESE WORDS in a sermon given in
June of 1942 at Church of St. Mary the Virgin in Oxford. It was
later published under the title *The Weight of Glory* and has rightly
become one of the most famous and frequently reprinted sermons
of the twentieth century. In it, Lewis debunks the notion that a
good Christian should not be motivated by rewards. He acknowl-
edges that the New Testament has a lot to say about self-denial
and taking up our crosses to follow Christ but points out that
such statements never see self-denial as an end in itself. Instead,
self-denial is justified by the reward that it brings—the fulfillment
of our highest desires and deepest longings. As he put it,

If we consider the unblushing promises of reward and the staggering nature of the rewards promised in the Gospels, it would seem that Our Lord finds our desires, not too strong, but too weak. We are half-hearted creatures, fooling about with drink and sex and ambition when infinite joy is offered us, like an ignorant child who wants to go on making mud pies in a slum because he cannot imagine what is meant by the offer of a holiday at the sea. We are far too easily pleased.[1]

What Lewis helps us see is that though God calls us to follow him, and genuine following involves genuine sacrifice, such sacrifices do not go unrewarded. Therefore, if we are arguing that Christians should take on the identity of followers and embrace it wholeheartedly, it is only right that we should also identify the rewards one can expect for doing so.

It is particularly important to consider rewards when discussing followership. In part, this is because the rewards of leadership are so obvious and so deeply embedded in our common cultural understanding of leadership. Leadership brings affirmation, respect, money, power, fame, and fulfillment. Leading also appears to be its own reward, the equivalent of winning a game rather than losing it, of success rather than failure. Followership, on the other hand, is perceived to be the opposite. It is not rewarded because it is seen as a sort of failure. One might even say it would be wrong to honor or reward followership in the same way that it would be wrong to honor or reward bad grades: we should not incentivize bad behavior or underachieving. Furthermore, follow-

---

1   C. S. Lewis, *The Weight of Glory and Other Addresses*, ed. Walter Hooper (Harper Collins: New York, 2001), 26.

ership sounds restrictive, confining, and burdensome. It certainly does not sound like it could be its own reward. At best, we might stretch our imagination enough to think that followership might be like spinach—it tastes bad but it is rumored to be good for you.

But this entire line of thought is mistaken.

We will argue in this chapter that followership is exactly the sort of thing that should be, and ultimately is, rewarded. It is rewarding for individuals and for organizations. It is its own reward, and it is also rewarded externally. Most importantly, followership is rewarded by God and he delights and finds joy in our following. All in all, the rewards of following are grossly underestimated—not just because there really are rewards to following that we usually don't see but also because upon seeing them, we discover them to be some of the greatest rewards we could ever imagine.

## Rewards for Oneself

We have already studied the abundance of parables Jesus gave on the theme of masters and servants. In all of these, we noted the common theme that revolves around a servant giving an account to his master. The particular job that a servant is called to do varies widely, and sometimes that job may include leading or giving oversight. However, from the standpoint of the parables, the servant is always viewed as a follower—one who is subordinate to and who answers to his master. The servant is not setting the agenda but rather following the commands of the master or vineyard owner or king. The climax of the parable is always the judgment scene where the master assesses the efforts of the servant and deems the servant faithful or unfaithful. But the other consistent theme in all these parables is that they are about rewards. In almost every instance, the parable ends with an accounting that includes a reward for the good and faithful servant. The reward varies. Sometimes it is financial, other times it is expanded stewardship or entering into rest or the heavenly kingdom. But one of the most common rewards is simply the declaration that the servant has pleased the master. The faithful servant hears the voice of the master say, "Well done, thou good and faithful servant!" (Matt. 25:21 KJV).

The power of such a reward should not be underestimated. I (Rick) confess it is hard for me to hear those words without feeling a lump in my throat or a tear in my eye. The great British preacher Charles Spurgeon puts it far more eloquently than I ever could when he writes,

With what infinite delight will Jesus fill our hearts if . . . we are happy enough to hear Him say, "Well done, good and faithful servant." Oh, if we shall hold on to the end despite the temptations of Satan . . . and all the entanglements of the world! Oh, if we can keep our garments unspotted from the world, preaching Christ according to our measure of ability and winning souls for Him, what an honor it will be! What bliss to hear Him say, "Well done!" The music of these two words will have Heaven in them to us. How different it will be from the verdict of our fellow men who are often finding fault with this and that, though we do our best. We never could please them, but we have pleased our Lord! . . . He sets all right by saying, "Well done!" Little will it matter, then, what all the rest have said—neither the flattering words of friends nor the harsh condemnations of enemies will have any weight with us when He says, "Well done!"[2]

This is the eternal and divine version of the delight we see in our children when they succeed in pleasing us. We exclaim, "Good job, Johnny!" and Johnny's face shines incandescent with delight at having pleased us. How much more will we feel that delight when Jesus regards our efforts and proclaims, "Well done!"

A second personal reward we receive for faithful following is intrinsic to successful followership itself and is something received in the here and now: the reward of living under the easy yoke that Christ promises to his followers. This easy yoke was described in the previous chapter, but the significance of the reward it offers deserves more attention. It is not a reward for on-the-spot efforts to turn the other cheek or go the extra mile or obey some particular teaching of Christ. Rather, the reward is the natural result of following Christ as an ongoing lifestyle. It causes the reordering of one's affections, activities, and aspirations so that they coincide with his will and are pleasing to his heart. Dallas Willard explains this well:

> We so devoutly believe in the power of effort-at-the-moment-of-action alone to accomplish what we want [that we] completely ignore the need for character change in our lives as a whole. . . . We intend what is right, but we avoid the life that would make it reality. . . . So, ironically, in our efforts to avoid the necessary pains of discipline we miss the easy yoke and light

2   Charles Spurgeon, "Unprofitable Servants," *Spurgeon's Sermons Volume 26: 1880*, https://www.ccel.org/.

burden. We then fall into the rending frustration of trying to do and be the Christian we know we ought to be without the necessary insight and strength that only discipline can provide.[3]

Merely attempting to obey on the spot, then, is doomed to fail and will only lead to frustration. Such efforts are not their own reward but rather their own punishment! This punishment does not result from divine intervention but rather is a natural consequence of failing to make following Jesus the overarching pattern of our lives. We refuse to apprentice ourselves to him and his lifestyle but still think that we can imitate his behaviors. Willard goes on to explain that

> Jesus never expected us simply to turn the other cheek, go the second mile, bless those who persecute us, give unto them that ask, and so forth. These responses [are] rightly understood to be characteristics of Christlikeness [but] were set forth by him as illustrative of what might be expected of a new kind of person—one who intelligently and steadfastly seeks, above all else, to live within the rule of God. . . . Jesus did invite people to follow him into that sort of life from which behavior such as loving one's enemies will seem like the only sensible and happy thing to do.[4]

Perhaps an analogy would help. I (Rick) spent a lot of time skiing while growing up in Colorado. I learned what might be called the rules of skiing: keep your weight on your downhill ski,

3  Dallas Willard, *The Spirit of the Disciplines* (HarperOne: New York, 1998), 6.
4  Willard, *The Spirit of the Disciplines*, 7.

bend your knees, lean away from the mountain, and keep your shoulders pointed downhill. For new skiers, these rules do not feel like an easy yoke. They feel awkward, counterintuitive, and extremely difficult to follow. If you lean away from the mountain you feel like you will fall head over heels all the way down the slope! It is far more natural to lean back toward the mountain so that falling just means a soft bump on the backside and a quick stop. I hated these rules when I was first learning how to ski. They seemed not only difficult but downright dangerous. But I wanted to learn to ski, so I ultimately apprenticed myself to these rules. Eventually I internalized them and they became second nature, and when that happened, I found myself liberated by the very same rules I once hated. I could turn my skis more easily. I could maintain control on increasingly steep slopes. Skiing became a delight. Following the rules was no longer a burden at all—they felt completely natural. Twenty years later, my daughter moved to Colorado and she wanted me to teach her how to ski. It was almost comical to see her frustration when I began telling her to bend her knees or lean away from the mountain. When the rules of skiing are internalized and habituated, they are liberating and very much their own reward. But before the rules are internalized and habituated, they are a terrible and irritating burden.

It is exactly this way with learning to be a follower of Christ. The disciplines of the spiritual life are hard at first, but they shape us into Christlikeness. As our life is more and more formed like Christ's, doing the things he did becomes second nature, or, more precisely, transformed nature. We also discover, similar to skiing, that as the disciplines are mastered, they make more sense and actually make a person happier and more fulfilled. For example, the discipline of confessing one's sins may be unpleasant and burdensome at the outset. However, as we continue to practice confession, we gain sensitivity to sin as well as a deeper appreciation for grace and forgiveness. As we savor forgiveness in our own life it becomes part of our nature and, as a result, it is much easier to forgive others as we ourselves have been forgiven. What sounds like a burdensome command becomes natural and easy because our souls have been reshaped. Ultimately, we obey countless commands simply because they seem natural and right within the pattern of life we have been living. The command often does not even come to mind, but we obey it nonetheless because it just seems to be the right thing to do at the moment. Our pattern of past decisions makes the next decision easier and more natural. The burden is light, the yoke is easy, and following has become its own reward.

Notice that "following" as we are discussing it here stretches far beyond any particular organizational or missional context. It is not simply a behavior offered to a particular leader. Rather, it is a mindset of following that manifests itself in organizational life but also every other aspect of our lives as well. Jesus is Lord of all, so our following of him pertains to all we do. Our lives are made up of a thousand tiny "follows"—little choices we make regarding the smallest matters that may not even register as reward worthy in our minds but are such in God's economy. The parable of the sheep and goats is a perfect example of this, as Jesus is rewarding believers who did tiny acts of care, so small that they don't even remember having done them (Matt. 25:37–40). Imagine God's voice of approval for hugging an unlovely or unlovable person, forgiving the undeserving, befriending the loner, valuing the forgotten, or encouraging the disappointed. God notices when we pray for a friend who has lost all hope and can no longer pray for themselves, when we sit in silence to comfort someone, and when we bring a meal to a grieving family. Our acts of following may be tiny but God notices them, and what he notices will not go unrewarded. He knows that our little acts of following today will equip us for bigger acts of following that lie ahead.

## Rewards for an Organization or Church

Effective followership benefits not only the individual follower but also the organization, church, or ministry of that follower. One of the best descriptions of these organizational rewards is found in the New Testament teachings about the church, particularly its discussions of spiritual gifts and the body of Christ. Though these passages use the language of member and head, this carries very similar connotations to leader and follower. The head is Christ himself, the members are followers of Christ, and together they make up the church, an organization (or organism), which is referred to as the "body of Christ." Members (followers) in these passages have two different kinds of relationships: relationships to other members and a relationship to the head. When these relationships are healthy, the body of Christ as a whole flourishes; when these relationships are disordered or unhealthy, the entire body suffers. To begin at the top, there is only one head, Christ (Eph. 4:15), and all the members are subordinate to him. The head sets the agenda for all of the members, apportioning gifts (Eph. 4:7; 1 Cor. 12:11), empowering their working (1 Cor. 12:11), directing their service (1 Cor. 12:5), and coordinating the activities (Eph. 4:16), all for the purpose of glorifying Christ and making him known (Eph. 4:13).

However, healthy relationships between the different members of the body can be difficult to achieve. In 1 Corinthians 12, Paul clearly reminds his readers that Christ is the head to which each member is attached, but much more of his attention is devoted to problems that have arisen between different members of the body. Paul is distressed because he sees some gifts being overvalued at the expense of others. This is causing jealousy, disunity, and division, and the body as a whole is suffering.

Paul addresses this problem by helping his readers think more clearly about what it means to be part of a body and, more particularly, what it means to be one member among many members that make up the body. First, Paul makes it clear that the well-being of the body depends on all members being equally valued. All members are valued because they bring a needed gift to the body. Though the gifts are different, they are all equally divine—they are all given by God and should all be honored as such. Furthermore, each gift is essential—the body as a whole needs each member because none of the members are complete in and of themselves. Paul puts it this way, "if the whole body were an ear, where would be the sense of smell?"(1 Cor. 12:17). No member is designed to do everything; we are to function in mutual dependence on one another. Since each member is needy (incomplete) and each member is needed (offering something essential), all members should be valued and honored. Paul says God's intention in all of this is that "there may be no division in the body, but that the members all have the same care for one another" (1 Cor. 12:24–25). Clearly, then, the biblical vision is that the church will flourish when members are performing their God-ordained function in harmony with those who perform other essential functions and when all members are equally valued.

One further comment is needed. In the body metaphors, Christ is the head and therefore the ultimate leader. Nonetheless, when Paul lists the gifts, he includes the gift of administration, or, as it is often translated, the gift of leadership. This structure fits perfectly with the understanding of leadership and followership we have been presenting throughout this book. We have consistently argued that everyone is a follower and that for certain people, faithful following means being a leader. They may or may not have a felt desire to lead, but they lead simply because God has appointed them to the task. Their following requires them to lead. In this passage, the same thing is happening, just expressed in the language of body, gifts, and members. Everyone is a member of the body, and every member is apportioned a gift. Some receive a gift of leadership, so they lead because faithfully using the gift demands it. They are still first and foremost a member of the body—a follower—and that never goes away. But the role they play as a member includes a leadership role, which they fill as a subordinate to Christ. These leaders are not autonomous, casting their own vision or creating their own mission. Instead, they have been appointed to help organize and coordinate the service of others around them.

Now we must return to the issue of rewards. The language of Ephesians 4:12–16, where Paul also takes up the body metaphor, is particularly vivid in this regard. Having identified the diversity of spiritual gifts, Paul notes that they all serve a single purpose: building up the body of Christ. In the healthy body, the cooperative working of the gifts enables the church to be united, to mature, to obtain the full stature of Christ, to no longer be children, to keep sight of the goal even in the face of wind and waves, to be wise enough to avoid deceitful schemes, to grow up into Christ the head, to allow each member to work properly, and finally, to build up the body in love, the greatest of Christian virtues. What Paul offers here is an extensive description of the church as a flourishing organization. It is an organization that is unified, empowered, and structured around a shared mission, operating as a team, valuing each member's contributions, and supplying each member's needs. It is a wonderful place to be.

It is also striking how much of this description of a flourishing church also applies to other organizations—even those in the secular world. Robert Kelley's discussion of leadership and followership, which we considered in chapter two, offers a vision of an organization in which leadership and followership are working effectively together. In such cases, leaders and followers are filling different roles, but both are equally valued. In Kelley's words:

> We can think of [leading and following] as equal but different activities . . . people who are effective in the leader role have the vision to set corporate goals and strategies, the interpersonal skills to achieve consensus, the verbal capacity to communicate enthusiasm to large and diverse groups of individuals, the organizational talent to coordinate disparate efforts, and, above all, the desire to lead. People who are effective in the follower role have the vision to see both the forest and the trees, the social capacity to work well with others, the strength of character to flourish without heroic status, the moral and psychological balance to pursue personal and corporate goals at no cost to

either, and, above all, the desire to participate in a team effort for the accomplishment of some greater common purpose.[5]

The organization he envisions has a clear strategy: individuals using their diverse gifts and talents, valuing their colleagues, and working in a coordinated fashion to accomplish some greater purpose. It sounds remarkably similar to the words of Paul.

## Delighting God

From a biblical standpoint it is clear that we can offer nothing to God that he hasn't first given to us (1 Chron. 29:14). Romans 11:35 states, "Who has given a gift to him that he might be repaid?" Yet, God does find delight in our following.

To think about how our following is received by God, let us return to the comments we already made about the rewards that we receive as individuals. The first of those rewards was the joy of being praised by God and hearing him say, "Well done, thou good and faithful servant!" (Matt. 25:21 KJV). We likened this to the joy that a child feels when praised by a parent. This is an apt metaphor, since it also invites us to think about how joyful a parent feels when they have an opportunity to give their child such robust praise. For all of us who have been parents, one of the greatest joys we feel is when one of our children does something truly praiseworthy. Similarly, God delights in moments when we have earned his praise. The fact that all we can offer him is what he gave us to begin with does not diminish his joy in the least. The same is often true of human parents and children as well.

5   Robert E. Kelley, "In Praise of Followers," *Harvard Business Review* 66, no. 6 (December 1988): 146–47.

We may have taught our child the Bible verse they so proudly recited; we may have given them the money they shared with a needy friend. But this fact in no way diminishes our joy when we see them perform these activities.

God also finds joy in seeing us walk in his ways, accomplish the tasks he has appointed for us, and shine our lights in such a way that others glorify him. Consider the following passage of Scripture:

> Thus says the LORD: "Heaven is my throne, and the earth is my footstool; what is the house that you would build for me, and what is the place of my rest? All these things my hand has made, and so all these things came to be, declares the LORD. *But this is the one to whom I will look: he who is humble and contrite in spirit and trembles at my word.* (Isa. 66:1–2)

In this passage, the Lord poses a rhetorical question. In fact, he is asking the question that we have just been discussing: "What can we possibly offer to God?" In this case, he asks if we could build him a house or a place he could rest. Obviously, the answer is no. Building a house for God is completely impossible since heaven is God's throne, earth is his footstool, and all things in between have already been made by his hands. What could we possibly offer? His answer is simply that we can offer him a humble and contrite spirit. It is people like that who draw God's attention; all the grand aspirations for a building project are irrelevant. It is the posture of the heart that pleases God and draws him near (Isa. 57:15).

A slightly different way to delight God's heart is found in this passage from Jeremiah:

Thus says the LORD: "Let not the wise man boast in his wisdom, let not the mighty man boast in his might, let not the rich man boast in his riches, but let him who boasts boast in this, that he understands and knows me, that I am the LORD who practices steadfast love, justice, and righteousness in the earth. For in these things I delight, declares the LORD." (Jer. 9:23–24)

Here, Jeremiah is focusing more on seeking and knowing God rather than on the heart posture of contrition and humility, but the result is similar. God is pleased in both cases. In fact, there is a direct relationship between humility and knowing God. A heart posture of humility and contrition enables us to draw near to God so that we might know him. As Psalm 138:6 says, the Lord "regards the lowly, [but] the haughty he knows from afar." God delights in us as we draw near to him. It is also interesting that in both these cases, the qualities that are pleasing to God are character qualities that we much more commonly associate with followers than leaders. God is pleased by a spirit of lowliness, not of might; he is drawn to a heart of contrition rather than a visionary or charismatic spirit. Jeremiah 9 makes this even more explicit by listing attributes that sound exactly like what we might think of as the traits of leadership: wisdom, might, and riches. But these are not the qualities that delight God. Instead, God delights in those who know and understand him. It is clear from the rest of Jeremiah 9 that knowing and understanding are not merely intellectual but also practical. The problem that concerns Jeremiah is not that people have refused to learn God's laws; rather, he bemoans those who have forsaken the law by refusing to obey the commands or walk in his ways. God desires and delights in those who practice love, justice, and righteousness. He yearns for those who follow him rather than those who have "stubbornly followed their own hearts (Jer. 9:14)."

In short, it seems that the hallmarks of faithful following—qualities like humility, obedience, seeking God, and walking in his ways—are also qualities that God loves and delights in. In a sense, God finds our following rewarding!

## Conclusion

Followership is both demanding and rewarding. It is not a small matter to choose to follow Jesus, to take up one's cross, to put one's hand to the plough and never look back. Perhaps the most certain proof that such following is not a small matter is the size and nature of the rewards associated with it. Followership gives rewards in heaven and rewards on earth. It gives rewards for individuals and rewards for families, organizations, churches, and ministries. It gives rewards that are vast and eternal. It gives rewards that are personal and intimate. It gives rewards from the very lips of Jesus as well as the rewards of companionship and appreciation from our fellow followers. Our followership even delights God himself, who loves his followers. Let us therefore choose to follow with a zeal worthy of the rewards that await us.

# Conclusion

WRITING A BOOK ON FOLLOWERSHIP in a culture that is obsessed with leadership is a risky business. Not only do you run the risk of writing a book that doesn't sell well but also of offending people. At the very least, you run the risk of people thinking you are completely detached from reality. Long before this book ever came to press, we both had several experiences of explaining the topic of our book, only to have a person respond, "You are writing a book on *what?*"

It is our hope that as you have read these pages, you have come to share our conviction that a firm grip on reality is completely compatible with a robust commitment to followership. And hopefully you have also joined us in discovering that there is a lot more to followership than meets the eye. First, we must rethink the stubborn conceptual problem of a leadership-only world and acknowledge that if we have no followers, we cannot really have any leaders. We must also acknowledge, as studies have shown, that followership is actually essential to the flourishing of all human organizations. Likewise, we must accept the need to train and honor the contributions of followers. All this rethinking can be applied to leadership and followership regardless of one's worldview.

For Christians, however, we discovered several additional problems. How can we make sense of the words of Christ himself, who seemed to go to almost any extreme to portray himself as a follower? If he was so eager to take on this mantle, how can we refuse? Furthermore, the idea of discipleship itself—the most fundamental call of the Christian life—is intrinsically a followership notion. Discipleship is simply a call to follow Christ and nothing more. And although the world may have a disdain for the followership imagery of Scripture—sheep and servants and slaves and submission and obedience—surely Christians cannot share in that disdain. Each and every one of those attitudes and activities are commanded in the New Testament and modelled by Christ and the apostles. And, of course, good followership is far more demanding and rewarding than it might appear. It is demanding because it is grounded in a wholehearted commitment to a mission and the person who that mission is about: Jesus and his kingdom. It is rewarding not only because God rewards those who answer his call but also because the life of a follower is really just the life of the easy yoke that Christ promises to all who come to him.

So we hope that you will join us on the journey of following. We hope that you put your hand to the plough, take up your cross, and follow Jesus. And in so doing, we hope you will also find delight in the companionship of countless others who have answered the same call. Many of them will run beside you as you persevere in the race that is set before you. Others will have gone ahead of you, creating the path you now follow. And you may be encouraged to hear their voices as part of a great cloud of witnesses that cheer you on. Further, there are the many, many people who will be coming behind you. For these folks who are just deciding to follow, it is the impression of your footprints that will guide them in the way of Jesus. It is our prayer that you will find the journey both meaningful and joyful, and that most of all, at its end, you will hear the sacred and treasured words, "Well done, thou good and faithful servant!" (Matt. 25:21 KJV).

# Study Guide

WE MOST OFTEN THINK OF LEADING and following in vocational settings like work, or perhaps politics, business, or education. This book is not limited to those contexts, for all their
importance. We think following in our personal lives is also extremely important—even when it feels far removed from a paid
job or a publicly celebrated calling.

Therefore, the reflection and discussion questions in this study
guide deal with leading and following. But they do not just apply
to paid jobs. They apply to any place where you are making things
happen in and around other people. They apply to soccer moms
who feel like they are constantly shuttling around a batch of young
children. They apply to retired people who have opportunities to
make all kinds of things happen, though they likely won't be paid
for it. These questions apply to teachers who teach but also those
who lead committees and sit on committees and sometimes feel
like committees are sitting on them. They apply to students who
are often sitting in classrooms (and who may or may not be doing
anything) but also to students joining clubs, playing sports, and
working part- or full-time jobs. They apply to CEOs who thought

being in the corner suite meant that they were finally calling the shots—until they had their first board meeting. They also apply to CEOs who thought they would finally be dealing with all the big decisions and instead are spending their days dealing with well-paid adults who squabble like preschoolers in a sandbox. They apply to elected officials who have dreams for the community they serve and to their staff who actually have to do the things that keep the existing community running. It applies to all of us. We live every day in a jungle of getting things done with people above and below and right beside us—people who may or may not be helping. We act, choose, lead, and follow—and as Christians we hope, in all our doings, to enthrone Christ as King in every aspect of the created order and in every sphere of human endeavor.

These study questions will help a reader both understand and apply the material found in each chapter. We strongly encourage you to read and discuss these questions with other friends and colleagues who share your interest in becoming more faithful and God-pleasing followers. May God bless your time of reflection!

## Chapter 1

In addition to reflecting on chapter 1 of the book, the following questions will also ask you to identify three life settings that will serve as the ongoing focus of the study guide as a whole. We encourage you not to rush through this process but rather identify such life settings in a prayerful and reflective manner.

1. Identify three important life settings that God has placed you in right now. These will serve as the places in which you seek to be a more faithful follower. A few thoughts about life settings:

- By a life setting, we simply mean a context in which you are regularly doing things that you find meaningful or necessary.
- Make sure that these matter to you right now, whether or not they matter to others. They may not be the biggest things you are involved in, but they should be things that tug at your heart. (It might be a demanding job, a needy child, a class you are taking, or a church group you are leading or participating in.)

a. Life setting #1:

-----

-----

b. Life setting #2:

-----

-----

c. Life setting #3:

-----

-----

- As you think of the life settings you find yourself in, briefly describe any tensions you are feeling about leading and following.

-----

-----

-----

-----

2. For each situation, identify

   • The parts of this situation that you believe to be your responsibility and the parts that are the responsibility of others
   • Your major concerns, anxieties, hopes, dreams, or plans for that life setting

   ---------------------------------------------------------------

   ---------------------------------------------------------------

   ---------------------------------------------------------------

   ---------------------------------------------------------------

3. Take a few moments to pray for each of these life settings and list anything about the situation that the Holy Spirit seems to bring to mind.

   ---------------------------------------------------------------

   ---------------------------------------------------------------

   ---------------------------------------------------------------

   ---------------------------------------------------------------

4. Write a single word that might capture what you are feeling for each situation (e.g., wait, trust, persevere, change, leap, rest, rejoice, kneel, initiate).

   ---------------------------------------------------------------

   ---------------------------------------------------------------

   ---------------------------------------------------------------

   ---------------------------------------------------------------

5. Take a few moments to pray through each of these life settings, asking God to help you understand why he has called you to this place and what he might have you do.

---

---

---

---

## Chapter 2

1. Consider the stereotypes of following that you have in your own mind. Which of those mentioned in the chapter do you most resonate with and why?

---

---

---

---

2. What are the best and worst aspects of following in your current life settings?

---

---

---

---

3. Identify ways in which you are (or could be) mission-centric in your thoughts about your current life situations. Also consider whether you are drawn to be leader-centric in any of these settings.

------------------------------------------

------------------------------------------

------------------------------------------

------------------------------------------

4. How well do the demands of your current leadership structure fit with your perceived sense of mission and calling?

------------------------------------------

------------------------------------------

------------------------------------------

------------------------------------------

5. Think about your current life settings individually. For each setting, identify which of the following aspects is most needed and why:

- clearer direction

------------------------------------------

------------------------------------------

- an attitude adjustment

------------------------------------------

------------------------------------------

- an energy infusion

- a patience supplement

- a major course correction

6. As you think through each of these areas, identify what part you can play in meeting that need and what should be done by others.

## Chapter 3

1. What do you think the relationship is between becoming a mature Christian and becoming a leader?

2. How do you feel about the description of Jesus as a follower? Does this fit with your own perception of Jesus? Why or why not?

3. This chapter identified certain aspects of the call Jesus gave to his followers: his call was urgent, demanding, and personal. Briefly consider each of these aspects in your own experience.

- How has the call of Christ seemed urgent in your own experience? If it has not seemed urgent, does this make you feel left out or relieved?

- Identify any important things that following Jesus has demanded of you and describe how you have responded to these demands.

- Has Jesus's call seemed personal to you or have you experienced it more generally (i.e., as a call that went out to all and you just happened to answer)?

- Have you experienced times where you were simply unable to do something you really wanted to do because of the call to follow Jesus?

4. Describe your followership chain. Who is in front of you that you can watch and imitate as an aid to following Christ himself? Who is behind you, watching and learning from you?

5. How clearly do you see Jesus through those who are leading you? Identify specific examples.

6. How clearly do you show Jesus to those who follow you? Try to specifically identify what you hope they see you modeling.

-------------------------------------------------------------------------

-------------------------------------------------------------------------

7. How has followership been perceived in the organizations, churches, or ministries you have been a part of? How does this correlate with biblical teaching and how does it resonate with your own soul?

-------------------------------------------------------------------------

-------------------------------------------------------------------------

-------------------------------------------------------------------------

-------------------------------------------------------------------------

## Chapter 4

1. Imagine that you are right now sitting down with Jesus face-to-face over a cup of coffee and hearing him explain to you that he has prepared all of the different life settings you find yourself in—giving you leadership responsibilities in some and followership responsibilities in others—and he is now giving you a chance to ask him questions about it.

   • What would you ask Jesus about? What seems confusing, surprising, or just plain wrong about your current life settings?

-------------------------------------------------------------------------

-------------------------------------------------------------------------

-------------------------------------------------------------------------

-------------------------------------------------------------------------

- What would you particularly like to thank or praise him for and why?

2. Suppose Jesus goes on to say that nothing is perfect in any of these settings and that is why he put you there (to make things better as a leader or follower), and then prompts you to think about how you might make your little corner of this world shine with the light of the next. What would you say about each of your life settings if Jesus asked you to walk him through them and tell him your plans?

3. With this conversation in mind, what are some actions you could take in the near future that would make one of your life settings just a little bit better?

4. Conclude your reflections by praying for resources, insights, or interventions that you really need in order to do what you believe God is calling you to do.

-------------------------------------------------------------

-------------------------------------------------------------

-------------------------------------------------------------

-------------------------------------------------------------

## Chapter 5

1. Kuyper's congregation spoke up to call him back to biblical and theological fidelity. They did it in a persistent and thoughtful way over the course of many small group meetings. What concerns do you have today about the biblical fidelity of your church or ministry or family members? How have you engaged these issues and is there anything you need to learn from the example of Kuyper's congregation?

-------------------------------------------------------------

-------------------------------------------------------------

-------------------------------------------------------------

-------------------------------------------------------------

2. Some of the worst imaginable life circumstances were experienced by the people in and around the village of Le Chambon. The Jews in particular were victims of some of the most grievous violations of human rights in the entire twentieth century—but those who chose to help them commonly experienced the same fate. Nonetheless, the ordinary church members in Le Chambon responded with a

calm, consistent, active resistance. Their lack of angry outrage seems very different than our responses today. I've seen many social media posts arguing about current events that exhibit a stronger sense of outrage than any complaints spoken by the Christ followers in Le Chambon. What do you think accounts for this difference?

3. Compare and contrast what is demanded of membership in your current church setting with the practices of the Church of the Saviour in Washington, DC. Is there anything you would like to change about your current setting?

4. Are there any proddings of conscience that you have been ignoring or refusing to speak up about because you are not sure your comments will be well received? How might you engage these issues, even if you share some of Puddleglum's sense of inadequacy?

-------------------------------------------------------------

-------------------------------------------------------------

5. For the most part, followers live, work, and breathe in anonymity. Their names never go up in lights. When do you find yourself most longing for recognition, and in what circumstances are you most at peace with your level of acknowledgment?

-------------------------------------------------------------

-------------------------------------------------------------

-------------------------------------------------------------

-------------------------------------------------------------

## Chapter 6

1. Do some of your life settings seem mundane or ordinary? If so, where do you see Christ within these settings? What are some factors that make it hard to see him at present?

-------------------------------------------------------------

-------------------------------------------------------------

-------------------------------------------------------------

-------------------------------------------------------------

2. Imagine you were written into one of the master-follower parables that Jesus told. Briefly describe who your masters would be right now, what they are asking of you, and how you are responding.

3. Imagine the moment when you stand before Jesus to give an account for your stewardship. What do you think he will say? Is there anything you would feel the urge to explain to him before he passed judgment?

4. It is good to think through each of your life settings and identify what you actually are responsible for. You might be in a dysfunctional family, classroom, business, church, or nation. Perhaps you are not the leader. Nonetheless, God has placed you there and you have certain abilities and responsibilities. God may not hold you accountable as a parent, boss, teacher, pastor, or president, but he will hold you accountable as a child, worker, student, church member, or citizen. We want to live without regrets wherever God has placed us. Identify at least two life situations that seem particularly important to you right now.

- What is he asking of you and how are you doing?

- What can you do, or avoid doing, that would help make things just a little bit better?

## Chapter 7

1. As you think through your important life settings, what character qualities are most needed in each one and how do those match with the character you actually possess?

2. If you could work on acquiring one particular virtue in greater measure, what would it be and why?

3. What soul rhythms are you most interested in putting into practice? Identify what you would like to do to get started in this rhythm. (Feel free to adjust, alter, or add to the list of soul rhythms given in this chapter.)

4. What soul rhythms feel most natural to you? What can you do to enhance and deepen your practice of these disciplines?

5. Are there any of these soul rhythms that you find yourself resisting or wanting to ignore? If so, why?

------------------------------------------------------------

------------------------------------------------------------

## Chapter 8

1. Describe a reward that might come to you from each of your life settings. If nothing comes to mind, you might think of things that you are currently doing that are sacrificial, dangerous, difficult, or demanding. What would fitting rewards be in your mind?

------------------------------------------------------------

------------------------------------------------------------

------------------------------------------------------------

------------------------------------------------------------

2. Imagine Jesus watching you within the midst of your daily activities in your current life settings. Suppose you could sit down and chat with him after a day in which he was following you around. What would you say to him, and what would he say to you?

------------------------------------------------------------

------------------------------------------------------------

------------------------------------------------------------

------------------------------------------------------------

3. If you have a setting that, at present, only evokes negative images and emotions with little or no prospect of reward, what is one

thing that you might start doing differently to turn things around and to increase the likelihood of a reward-worthy outcome?

-------------------------------------------------------------

-------------------------------------------------------------

-------------------------------------------------------------

-------------------------------------------------------------

# General Index

Aaron, 83
Abraham, 28

Bennis, Warren, 16
Berg, David, 37
Biden, Joe, 78–79, 100
Bonhoeffer, Dietrich, 135

Calvin, John, 83
Capitol Building
  attack on, 78
Chaleff, Ira, 96
Chambers, Oswald, 146–47
Christlikeness, 44, 153, 169, 180, 181
Christians, 28, 55, 70, 164, 192
  and followership, 17–18
Church of the Saviour, 115–28
Churchill, Winston, 98–99
citizenry/citizens, 78, 80, 85, 96, 112, 172
Collins, Jim, 27, 98
Colson, Chuck, 101–2
confession, 167–68
Cosby, Gordon, 116–19, 120–22
Cosby, Mary, 116

Cosper, Mike, 93–94
Crouch, Andy, 86–87

David, 28, 49, 139–40
disciples (of Jesus), 61, 62, 65–69
  as followers, 68
disciples (modern), 18, 20, 30, 63
discipleship, 70, 72, 117–18, 192
  *See also* Jesus Christ, and his call
    to discipleship
Driscoll, Mark, 85, 93

Elliot, Jim, 129–30
evangelicals, 87, 97
Ezekiel, 49

followers, 43, 76
  and the American church, 85–88
  being a follower after Christ's
    own heart, 136–37
  of Christ, 183
  description of an effective fol-
    lower, 142–43, 144–45
  distinction between leaders and
    followers, 39–40
  metaphors of followers, 47–48,
    53, 55

followership, 107, 124–25, 176–77, 190, 191–93
  academic studies of, 16
  biblical followership, 56
  Christian thought concerning, 40
  definitions of, 38–41
  faithful followership, 88–90, 94–106
  leader-centric followership, 42
  and leadership, 41–43, 84–85
  and the lordship of Christ, 73–76
  mission-centric followership, 42–43
  misunderstandings of, 44–47, 52–55
  stereotypes of, 37–38, 40, 43–44, 56
  traditional notions of, 16–17
  followership images are unattractive, 47–52
French, David, 102

Gideon, 33
God, 28–29, 41, 104, 105, 164–65, 182–84
  communication with, 169–70
  delighting God, 187–90
  faithfulness of, 139
  friendship with, 172–73
  gifts of, 170
  goodness of, 139
  grace of, 32, 146, 165, 170
  presence of, 152
  work of in the world, 43
  *See also* God's word
God's word, 155–60

Habakkuk, 84
Hallie, Phillip, 112, 113
Herman, Nicholas, 131–32
Hollander, E. P., 45–46

Holy Spirit, 121, 122, 153, 156, 157–58, 159, 172
  regeneration through, 150
hospitality, 171–73
Huguenots, 112
humility, 166–71

imitation, 68–73
"In Praise of Followership" (Kelley), 46–47
"informational malnourishment," 100
Israel, suffering of, 28–29

James, 62
Jeremiah, 33, 188–89
Jesus Christ, 41, 59–60, 72–73, 109, 136, 150–51, 180, 193
  and his call to discipleship, 65–68
  as follower, 60–65
  gifts of, 185
  as the incarnate Christ, 62, 64
  lordship of, 73–76, 182
  servant parables of, 137–41, 146–48, 177–78
  as a servant, 64–65
  teaching of, 179
  willingness of to take the place of one who serves, 63
John, 62, 63
Jones, Laurie Beth, 75
Jordyn, Betsy, 29–30
Judah, 84

Kellerman, Barbara, 17, 54–55
Kelley, Robert, 46–47, 53–54, 55, 140–41
  description of an effective follower, 142–43
  on leadership, 186–87
Kuyper, Abraham, 110–11, 123–28

Le Chambon, 111–15, 123–24
leaders, 84–85, 86–88, 96, 97, 189,
    191
  Christian leaders, 85, 103, 116
  bad leaders, 77
  the best leaders, 27, 28
  biblical leaders, 33, 34
  celebrity leaders, 97
  distinction between leaders and
    followers, 39–40
  effective leaders, 46
  established leaders, 50–51
  evangelical leaders, 85–86
  evil leaders, 78
  good leaders, 54, 88, 91
  as a judgment on followers,
    82–85
  organizational leaders, 99
  potential leaders, 15
  religious leaders, 101–2
  servant-leaders, 19
leadership, 36–37, 59, 107,
    186–87
  affirmations of, 74–75
  approaching leadership with cau-
    tion, 25
  assumptions about bad leaders,
    77–78
  the proper place of in human
    organizations, 23–24
  danger of leadership becoming an
    idol, 24
  definitions of, 30–31
  followership/leadership connec-
    tions, 84–85
  harmful statements concerning,
    29–31, 31–36
  helpful statements concerning,
    26–29
  nuanced view of, 25

popular leadership, 74
quality and nature of, 84
similarity of to money, 24
unintentional leadership,
    70–71
virtues of, 25
Lewis, C. S., 124–27, 175–76
Luther, Martin, 105, 129

Mars Hill Church, 93
Merton, Thomas, 133–34
mission
  internalizing a mission statement,
    95–96
  organizations seeking a mission,
    20
  owning your mission, 94–98
  sense of, 19
money, 23, 24
Moore, Russell, 90
Morgan, Jacob, 30
Morris, Leon, 63
Moses, 28, 33, 83

New Testament Epistles, 50
  the Pastoral Epistles, 71–72
Nichols, Tom, 79, 80

O'Connor, Elizabeth, 115, 119
Olsen, Ted, 89, 99

Pastor Trocmé, 114–15
Paul, 50–51, 70, 71, 76, 105, 109,
    169
  on the body metaphor,
    185–86
  on the incarnate Christ, 64
Peter, 73, 105
polarization/anger
  in modern times, 77
Puritans, 160

General Index

Razi Zacharias International Ministries (RZIM), 92

Saint Lawrence, 130–31, 132–33, 135
Samuel, 28
servanthood, 50, 51, 52, 63–64
Shepard, Thomas, 159–60
slothfulness, 142
soul rhythms, 150, 151–53, 161–64, 173–74
spiritual disciplines, 181–82
Spurgeon, Charles, 178
Stetzer, Ed, 87, 97
Stirewalt, Chris, 100–101
Stockdale Paradox, 98–99

Stonestreet, John, 78–79, 80, 85

Taylor, Daniel, 105–6
theology, 15, 170
    Christian, 82
    liberal, 110–11
    public, 96–97

virtue(s), 136, 149
    Christian, 186
    of leadership, 25
    public virtue, 81

Warren, Tish Harrison, 18–19
Willard, Dallas, 179–80
Wolff, Hans W., 138–39

# Scripture Index

**Genesis**
3 . . . . . . . . . . . . . . . . . 145

**Exodus**
32:1 . . . . . . . . . . . . . 83
32:7 . . . . . . . . . . . . . 83
32:9 . . . . . . . . . . . . . 83
32:11 . . . . . . . . . . . . 83
32:21 . . . . . . . . . . . . 83
32:22 . . . . . . . . . . . . 83
32:24 . . . . . . . . . . . . 83
32:25 . . . . . . . . . . . . 83
32:30 . . . . . . . . . . . . 83
33:14 . . . . . . . . . . . . 158

**Deuteronomy**
8:2 . . . . . . . . . . . . . . . 83

**1 Samuel**
8:4–22 . . . . . . . . . . 84

**1 Chronicles**
29:14 . . . . . . . . . . . . 187

**Psalms**
16:11 . . . . . . . . . . . . 158
23 . . . . . . . . . . . . . . . 49
23:4 . . . . . . . . . . . . . 140

23:6 . . . . . . . . . . . . . 139
31:20 . . . . . . . . . . . . 158
138:6 . . . . . . . . . . . . 189
139:16 . . . . . . . . . . 157
145:16 . . . . . . . . . . 146

**Proverbs**
4:23 . . . . . . . . . . . . . 151
17:24 . . . . . . . . . . . . 158
30:8 . . . . . . . . . . . . . 24

**Isaiah**
30:20–21 . . . . . . . . 149
42:1–4 . . . . . . . . . . 64
49:1–6 . . . . . . . . . . 64
50:4–9 . . . . . . . . . . 64
52:13—53:12 . . . 64
57:15 . . . . . . . . . . . . 188
66:1–2 . . . . . . . . . . 188

**Jeremiah**
9:14 . . . . . . . . . . . . . 190
9:23–24 . . . . . . . . . 153, 189
17:9 . . . . . . . . . . . . . 166

**Ezekiel**
18:30 . . . . . . . . . . . . 145

34................49, 82
34:23............49

*Habakkuk*
1:12..............84

*Matthew*
4:19..............67
4:23–25..........65
7:11..............170
10:8..............174
10:34–36........66
10:38............66
11:28–29........158
16:24............66
18:33............174
19:27–30........67
19:29............66
20:1–16..........143
20:28............174
24:36............141
24:42............141
25:12............141
25:14–30........141
25:21............76, 103, 178, 187,
                193
25:24–30........143
25:37–40........182
25:40............20, 113

*Mark*
8:34..............66
10:40............63
10:45............174
14:31............66

*Luke*
9:23..............66
9:59–61..........65
12:35–40........137
12:41–48........140

12:45............144
14:27............66
17:9..............146
17:10............146
15:11–32........143
17:7–10..........145
18:1–8..........143
19:12–27........141
19:21–27........143

*John*
5:19..............61
5:36..............61
6:38..............61
7:16..............61
8:26..............61
8:28..............61
8:42..............61
10................48, 49
10:4–5..........67
10:5..............48
10:8..............48, 67
10:10............48
10:14–16........67
10:18............61
10:29............61
11:16............66–67
12:25–26........23, 66
12:49............61
13:20............61
13:37............67
14:10............61
14:26............157
14:31............61
15:9..............61
15:10............61
16:13............157

*Acts*
10:36............73

# Scripture Index

**Romans**
6:2–6 . . . . . . . . . . . . 166
6:17 . . . . . . . . . . . . . 150
8:28 . . . . . . . . . . . . . 170
8:29 . . . . . . . . . . . . . 170
11:35 . . . . . . . . . . . . 187
12:2 . . . . . . . . . . . . . 105
12:17 . . . . . . . . . . . . 105
13:1 . . . . . . . . . . . . . 41
13:3–4 . . . . . . . . . . 83
14:12 . . . . . . . . . . . . 145
15:7 . . . . . . . . . . . . . 174

**1 Corinthians**
book of . . . . . . . . . . 102
2:11 . . . . . . . . . . . . . 157
3:5 . . . . . . . . . . . . . . 50
3:9–17 . . . . . . . . . . 103
3:21–23 . . . . . . . . . 50
4:7 . . . . . . . . . . . . . . 170
4:9–13 . . . . . . . . . . 103
4:10–12 . . . . . . . . . 103
6:11 . . . . . . . . . . . . . 153
11:1 . . . . . . . . . . . . . 70
12:5 . . . . . . . . . . . . . 183
12:11 . . . . . . . . . . . . 183
12:17 . . . . . . . . . . . . 184
12:24–25 . . . . . . . . 184

**2 Corinthians**
1:3–4 . . . . . . . . . . . . 174
4:15 . . . . . . . . . . . . . 168
5:18 . . . . . . . . . . . . . 174
5:20 . . . . . . . . . . . . . 173
11:7–33 . . . . . . . . . 73
12:9 . . . . . . . . . . . . . 170

**Galatians**
1:10 . . . . . . . . . . . . . 101
2:20 . . . . . . . . . . . . . 166
5:25 . . . . . . . . . . . . . 151

**Ephesians**
2:14 . . . . . . . . . . . . . 173
2:18–19 . . . . . . . . . 172
4:7 . . . . . . . . . . . . . . 183
4:12–16 . . . . . . . . . 185
4:13 . . . . . . . . . . . . . 183
4:15 . . . . . . . . . . . . . 183
4:16 . . . . . . . . . . . . . 183
5:11 . . . . . . . . . . . . . 89
5:20 . . . . . . . . . . . . . 169
6:6–7 . . . . . . . . . . . . 136

**Philippians**
2 . . . . . . . . . . . . . . . . 64
2:1–10 . . . . . . . . . . 73
3:8–10 . . . . . . . . . . 73
3:14 . . . . . . . . . . . . . 76
3:17 . . . . . . . . . . . . . 71

**Colossians**
3:13 . . . . . . . . . . . . . 174
3:15–17 . . . . . . . . . 169
3:22 . . . . . . . . . . . . . 140

**1 Thessalonians**
1:5–6 . . . . . . . . . . . . 70
1:8–9 . . . . . . . . . . . . 71
2:8 . . . . . . . . . . . . . . 70
2:14 . . . . . . . . . . . . . 71
5:2 . . . . . . . . . . . . . . 141
5:12–13 . . . . . . . . . 41

**2 Thessalonians**
2:13 . . . . . . . . . . . . . 153
3:9 . . . . . . . . . . . . . . 70

**2 Timothy**
2:2 . . . . . . . . . . . . . . 71
4:7 . . . . . . . . . . . . . . 147

**Titus**
2:12–13 . . . . . . . . . 141

**Hebrews**
6:12 .............. 70
12:1–3 ........... 147
13:7 ............. 29, 70, 71
13:17 ............ 29

**James**
1:17 .............. 170

**1 Peter**
2:23 .............. 105
5:3 ............... 70

**1 John**
4:19 .............. 174

**Revelation**
book of ........... 64